"The good and beautiful *me*—you've got to be kidding! My lifelong, toxic self-narrative has been a stubborn foe—like a petty dictator, no longer wanted yet refusing to stand down. Thank you, Jim, for patiently and carefully illuminating the path that leads to letting go of our common, neurotic need to create a self. And in letting go, to discover God's creation of our soul—which is the good and beautiful me."

Todd Hunter, Anglican bishop and author of *Deep Peace: Finding Calm in a World of Conflict and Anxiety*

"Cracking open the deep struggle of our human existence, Jim recovers the truth of our personhood—we are ensouled bodies seeking the transcendent. We long for God, and every false image we turn to erodes the truth of our being. Discover what false narratives have led you away from the truth of who you are in Christ—forgiven, redeemed, and holy—and follow the soul trainings for a deeper embrace of his love. Take care of your soul and allow Jim to guide you to the truth only found in Jesus."

Kyle Strobel, coauthor of *Where Prayer Becomes Real* and *The Way of the Dragon or the Way of the Lamb*

"More than most realize, the bottom level of discussions about many of the currents in our life is, Who are we? That is, anthropology. Jim Smith fulfills one of Dallas Willard's major hopes for the spiritual formation movement in this book—a Christian and biblical framing of who we are as persons, as souls. The danger of all such studies is self-idolatry, and that is why I so heartily recommend this book. Here we are called to understand ourselves as God created us and understands us and envelops us in Christ, that is, in his love and grace and transforming power."

Scot McKnight, professor of New Testament at Northern Seminary

"Writing in the venerable tradition of Dallas Willard and Richard Foster, James Bryan Smith has given us a valuable guide to caring for our souls in *The Good and Beautiful You*. Convinced that Christ is the way to the wellness of the soul, Smith points us to paths where we can find healing for our damaged souls. This book will help many people!"

Brian Zahnd, author of *When Everything's on Fire*

"With his signature combination of intellectual rigor, accessible language, and pastoral care, James Bryan Smith has helped thousands of us believe firmly in the goodness and beauty of God. But what are we to believe about ourselves? How do we fit into God's good and beautiful universe? Merging solid teaching and carefully crafted soul-training exercises, *The Good and Beautiful You* firmly debunks the false narratives we believe about ourselves and replaces them with life-giving, soul-enriching truth. This book is a treasure."

Richella J. Parham, author of *Mythical Me*

"James Bryan Smith writes what he lives, and no more so than in *The Good and Beautiful You*. With personal transparency, intellectual fullness, and day-to-day practicality, my friend Jim adds to what has already been a tremendous series of books on the Christian spiritual life. This book is a true and significant gift for any of us who walk with Jesus and tend to our souls."

Casey Tygrett, spiritual director and author of *As I Recall: Discovering the Place of Memories in the Spiritual Life*

"Six words come to mind whenever I think about my friend Jim: holy authenticity and intimacy with God. James Bryan Smith knows what it means to walk with God without pretense and with holy expectancy. He knows Jesus as his Redeemer, Healer, Defender, and Deliverer. Jim knows God; he knows his love. That's why he's just the person to write *The Good and Beautiful You*. Though we were born into sin, as Christ-followers we've been redeemed, through and through, by his grace. If you still struggle with a sense of identity and purpose, settle in and take your time working through these pages. I believe you'll encounter God, you'll hear his voice, and you'll learn afresh how much he loves you. Even today I pray that you hear the love song he sings over you, for it is life-giving and beautiful, just as Christ is in you."

Susie Larson, author of *Prevail* and host of *Susie Larson Live*

"Jim Smith takes us on a formation journey—his and simultaneously our own. We visit our false narratives so prevalent in the world today, and we are provided wider eyes to see the truth in every area of our being. Jim takes the key areas that we long for and invites us into the reality of the divine grace of God present to all of us. This is not a quick read unless, of course, that's all you long for. But if you are searching for riches out of the stones of your life, this book will help you see that you are the treasure you have been hoping for."

Juanita Campbell Rasmus, author of *Learning to Be*

james Bryan smith

The Good and Beautiful
YOU

DISCOVERING THE PERSON
JESUS CREATED YOU TO BE

An imprint of InterVarsity Press
Downers Grove, Illinois

InterVarsity Press
P.O. Box 1400, Downers Grove, IL 60515-1426
ivpress.com
email@ivpress.com

*InterVarsity Press® is the book-publishing division of InterVarsity Christian Fellowship/USA®,
a movement of students and faculty active on campus at hundreds of universities, colleges, and schools
of nursing in the United States of America, and a member movement of the International Fellowship
of Evangelical Students. For information about local and regional activities, visit intervarsity.org.*

Design: Cindy Kiple
Image: purple flower: © Yothin Sanchai / EyeEm / Getty Images

ISBN 978-0-8308-4694-8 (print)
ISBN 978-0-8308-4695-5 (digital)

Printed in the United States of America ∞

*InterVarsity Press is committed to ecological stewardship and to the conservation of natural resources
in all our operations. This book was printed using sustainably sourced paper.*

Library of Congress Cataloging-in-Publication Data

A catalog record for this book is available from the Library of Congress.

P	25	24	23	22	21	20	19	18	17	16	15	14	13	12	11	10	9	8	7	6	5	4	3	2	1
Y	38	37	36	35	34	33	32	31	30	29	28	27	26	25	24	23	22								

To Michael J. Cusick

For mining for a heart of gold and

being Jesus' accomplice in restoring my soul,

and

Fr. Adrian van Kaam

For his brilliant explanation of Christian theological

anthropology and its role in formation science,

and

Dr. Dallas Willard

For his brilliant insights into the

human person in *Renovation of the Heart*,

and

Richard J. Foster

For a living example of a good and beautiful life

and for the care and guidance of my soul.

contents

introduction

A few years after the first three books in the Good and Beautiful Series (*The Good and Beautiful God, The Good and Beautiful Life,* and *The Good and Beautiful Community*) were published, I was in England speaking on the book series. My friend Joe Davis and I had dinner one evening. Joe said to me, "The book series has been one of the most helpful tools I have used in ministry. Thank you for your work."

I thanked him for saying this. Then he said, "But you are missing *one* book."

"What book is missing?" I asked.

"*The Good and Beautiful You,*" Joe said.

"Why do you say this, Joe?"

"Because I have used the books with many groups, and while they have helped heal people's false *God narratives*—which is crucial—I have found that many Christians have very toxic *self-narratives,* which makes it difficult—even impossible—to progress in their lives."

I sat in silence for a while. In that moment I knew, intuitively, that Joe was right. I had assumed the *trilogy* was complete, but when he uttered those words, "the good and beautiful you," I knew there would come a day when I would need to write this book. But at the time Joe said this to me, I was not ready to write this book. There is an old saying I like: "When you are ready, the right book will find you." I think it is also true in writing: "When you are ready, the right book will emerge from you."

Over the next few years in my own journey, I would discover new, wonderful truths about my *identity*. Some of these truths were things I had known but had forgotten and suddenly they came to life again in my soul. David Brooks said that he writes, in part, "to remind myself of the kind of life I want to live." I suppose that is true of many of us who write. But in this case, it really happened. I was able, in writing this book, to rediscover the beauty and goodness of my own soul, and how my soul longs for things only God can provide. And I would learn that God, in Christ, has provided all of those things—for me, and for you. Writing this book has helped me to live the kind of life my soul has longed to live.

During the writing of this book, my mother and father-in-law, Penny and Emil Johnson, gave me a wonderful present. It is a framed print of one of my favorite sayings, "It is well with my soul." They gave it to me just as this book was coming together, and it gave me great joy to have something on the wall that reminded me of the importance of *wellness for our souls*. Now when I see it every day, I am grateful for the journey this book took me on, and what a joy it is to say each day, "It is well with my soul." Not because of anything I have done, but because God, who is good and beautiful, has provided everything our souls need.

BECOMING WHO YOU ARE IN CHRIST

Before my mentor, Dallas Willard, passed over to glory, I asked him what he thought about the rapid rise of the Christian spiritual formation movement. He said, "It is a wonderful thing, but my fear is the Christian spiritual movement will continue to grow so rapidly that the difficult work of establishing an *anthropological foundation* will not happen." By "anthropological foundation," Dallas was referring to a clear sense of the nature of the human person.

I asked, "Without an anthropological foundation, what will happen as a result?"

Dallas said, "The spiritual formation movement will degenerate into *technique*. It will focus on practices, and not on the soul."

My sense is that Dallas's prophecy has come true. Much of the teaching and writing on Christian spiritual formation focuses primarily on the disciplines—on the practices. And of course, the spiritual disciplines are wonderful tools in our formation. But why do we need a solid understanding of who we are in the process of spiritual formation? We need this foundation because Christian spiritual formation is not primarily about practices or the feelings they might engender. It is about becoming who you are in Christ. Walking a labyrinth or engaging in *lectio divina* can be powerful practices, but the practices themselves are not the point. Christian spiritual formation is not primarily about helping you feel more spiritual, but it is about forming you in Christ.

In short, the Christian faith is not primarily about belief and practices; it is primarily about what kind of people Christians become. And who we are, who we become, is a deep longing in our embodied souls. God designed us with a deep longing in our souls to be wanted, loved,

> The Christian faith is not primarily about belief and practices; it is primarily about what kind of people Christians become.

alive, and connected to God. In Christ, we are all of these and more. And when we live into this reality, we become the unique person God created us to be.

A writer who greatly influenced this book, Fr. Adrian van Kaam, once wrote,

I must become the unique person I am meant to be. The more I become what my Creator called me to be originally, the more I will be united with my divine origin. I must find my original self as hidden in God. The original life of a Christian, as St. Paul says, is hidden in Christ.

Our true self—our original self—the one created by and for Christ, the one made in the image of Christ, is hidden in Christ. Christian spiritual formation, then, is the process of allowing that original Christ-created Christ image to emerge. I have discovered that inviting the Spirit to help me become more like Jesus produces much better results than trying to be "the best version of myself." The practices we engage in are important in that they are means God uses, through the Spirit, to shape and form us. But we must never mistake the means for the ends.

MY HOPE FOR YOU

My hope for you as you read this book is that you will discover the good and beautiful you that Jesus created you to be. I pray that you will see yourself with wonder, see yourself as sacred—even though you are flawed and broken. I long for you to know that you are loved by God, forgiven for what you have done, and made alive by the power of Jesus' resurrection. I have written this book with the hope that you will see that you have a sacred story, a sacred body, and a sacred longing for God that is at your core. I hope and pray that you come to know your unique calling in this life and your divine destiny for glory in the next.

But there is one more desire I have for you as you read and engage with this book: that you will see your neighbor in the same way. I pray that you will look at those you interact with—your friends and coworkers and family members, as well as those people you disagree with politically or socially or culturally—as sacred beings, loved by God, who are worthy of your compassion and kindness because they, too, are of divine origin.

I wrote it because the series would not be complete without it. What was missing, as Joe pointed out, was a book that could help to correct the toxic self-narratives that are ruining so many lives. The true narrative about our identity, I discovered, cannot be disclosed by reason but only by revelation. Only God, through Christ, can reveal to us who we truly are. And in the end, what we discover—what I hope *you* discover—is that you are good and beautiful. In so doing, I pray that you will discover the person Jesus uniquely created you to be.

HOW to Get the most out of THIS BOOK

This book is intended to be used in the context of a community—a small group, a Sunday school class, or a few friends gathered in a home or coffee shop. Working through this book with others greatly magnifies the impact. If you go through this on your own, only the first four suggestions below will apply to you. No matter how you use it I am confident that God can and will accomplish a good work in you.

1. Prepare. Find a journal or notebook with blank pages.
You will use this journal to answer the questions sprinkled throughout each chapter and for the reflections on the soul-training experience found at the end of each chapter.

2. Read. Read each chapter thoroughly.
Try not to read hurriedly, and avoid reading the chapter at the last minute. Start reading early enough in the week so that you have time to digest the material.

3. Do. Complete the weekly exercise(s).

Engaging in exercises related to the content of the chapter you have just read will help deepen the ideas you are learning and will begin to mold and heal your soul. Some of the exercises will take more time to complete than others. Be sure to leave plenty of time to do the exercises before your group meeting. You want to have time not only to do the exercises but also to do the written reflections.

4. Reflect. Make time to complete your written reflections.

In your journal go through all the questions of each chapter. This will help you clarify your thoughts and crystallize what God is teaching you. It will also help with the next part.

5. Interact. Come to the group time prepared to listen and to share.

Here is where you get a chance to hear and learn from others' experiences and insights. If everyone takes time to journal in advance, the conversation in the group time will be much more effective. People will be sharing from their more distilled thoughts, and the group time will be more valuable. It is important to remember that we should listen twice as much as we speak! But do be prepared to share. The other group members will learn from your ideas and experiences.

6. Encourage. Interact with each other outside of group time.

One of the great blessings technology brings is the ease with which we can stay in touch. It is a good idea to send an encouraging email to at least two others in your group between meeting times. Let them know you are thinking of them, and ask how you can pray for them. This will strengthen relationships and deepen your overall experience. Building strong relationships is a key factor in making your experience a success.

one

You Have a Soul

Many years ago my mentor and friend, Richard J. Foster, and I had lunch. Not long into the lunch, Richard's face looked very serious, and he said, "I want you to hear this word, and take it to heart. Your career is going to change. You are going to move from the minor league to the major league in the next few years. *You must take care of your soul.*"

I said, "Well, I have no idea what that means, but . . . thanks for the advice."

"No, I am serious, Jim. You need to write this down and remember it."

So I wrote it down. I assumed Richard was just being nice; I never expected he might be right. I kept the napkin I wrote it on, but I did not heed his advice.

Richard was right. The next few years of my life, in terms of my career, changed. I went from being a college professor and part-time teaching pastor in a local church, to the head of a ministry with a growing number of staff. We were blessed with financial resources beyond our expectations, and we did our best to increase our impact for the kingdom of God. New opportunities came, and doors were opened that I had never dreamed of. I was traveling around the world, and it seemed clear that God was doing a lot of good through our work. I found myself feeling two things at once: excitement to do the work and enormous pressure to succeed.

I did what many people do: I poured my heart into it and worked harder than ever before. I read books on how to be a leader, studied ministry programs, learned about marketing and branding, and honed every skill I had in order to advance our work. Success kept coming, in terms of how success is measured in ministry work: more people were being reached and more influence was being exerted and more resources were being given. But I was enjoying it less and less.

I did not have a moral failure, I was not experiencing burnout, nor was I suffering under an addiction, though I suspect I had not sought help I could have. There was a lot of grief and unhealed trauma that I had suppressed. As a result, I simply lost joy and was suffering in silence. I made the common mistake of thinking that doing work for God was more important than caring for my own soul. And now I was paying the price, because my soul refused to be neglected. I had pursued and achieved success—but at what cost?

I confided my concerns with my longtime pastor and friend, Jeff, who said, "Maybe you need to talk to someone, a trusted counselor." I had never done any kind of therapy work, but I was desperate enough to try. God led me to a therapist in Colorado, and I set aside a week to go for some intensive counseling. I did not want to admit it, but I knew that I needed help. The only thing in my favor was a small amount of courage to ask for it. I knew that I would soon be going into the office of a therapist, and for the next week baring my soul.

"So," my therapist, Michael, asked, "What brings you here?"

"I cannot go on living this way," I said.

"Say more," he inquired.

"I feel empty inside. I have lost my joy, my smile. I just feel nothing," I said.

He invited me to share anything and everything I was comfortable sharing. I thought to myself, *Well, I am here, and it is safe, so I might as well let it all hang out.* I shared all of my biggest mistakes and regrets; I exposed all the skeletons in my closet; I confessed my worst sins and darkest fears, and the thoughts, words, and deeds of which I was most ashamed. This took around thirty minutes but felt like an eternity.

Michael sat in silence and listened, then said nothing for a minute. Then he said, "I am so impressed with your integrity. You are such a man of integrity."

"Wait, what? Did you not hear a thing I just said? I confessed my worst failures, most shameful sins, my darkest secrets, and your first response is that you are impressed with my *integrity*?"

"Yes, and it was such a joy and honor to hear it, not because you are *James Bryan Smith*, the author, but because you are Jim Smith, the wonderful human soul. In that confession, you were truly in alignment with God. The integrity I see in you is *not* because you named your struggle; the integrity is in your soul. You opened up your soul, the place no one can see, the place where there is pain and fear and shame, but there is also so much more that you do not see."

I was stunned.

"Jim," Michael said, looking right at me, "God sees into your soul—into the totality of who you are. Jesus looks at our worst and puts his arm around us and says, 'Well, *of course.*' Jesus knows the truth of where we are, and he does not condemn us for it. But he does have great expectancy for how much we can heal, for how free and alive we can be. It was an honor to see the core of your being. Right now, you only see the junk . . . I see the gold—*I see Christ in you.* Your soul is longing to be made well, and you have taken the first step toward that by coming here."

By the end of the week I felt like a new person. A burden had been lifted. On the last day, as I was leaving, I noticed for the first time that the name of the counseling program is Restoring the Soul. I suddenly thought of Richard, and what he had said many years earlier. I would learn that week and for the next few years that it was my soul, the thing years earlier Richard had asked me to guard, that was both the cause of my pain and the hope of my healing. I had, in fact, *not* guarded my soul. But now I would, and I resolved to try my best never to make that mistake again.

OUR SOULS WANT LIFE

Not long after my own time in therapy, I was listening to a podcast in which the guest spoke about his time in counseling. The guest was one of my favorite spiritual writers, whose books have been helpful to me. I was surprised to learn that he had struggled for years with clinical depression. He said he felt ashamed of his depression, feeling as if he had to keep it secret, and keeping the secret was exhausting. He assumed that the spiritual life was like an ascent to a high mountain where you try to touch God, but that spirituality had nothing to do with the valley and he had been living in the valley.

He said during his depression he never felt "less spiritual," but that the things he relied on in his life for meaning and purpose, such as his intellect and his emotional life, were gone; his willpower had been shattered. And yet, "there was this primitive core of being, this life force that was alive and holding out hope." He said it was his soul. He said, "The soul is this wild creature that knows how to survive where our intellect and our feelings and our will cannot." Then he said this: "Catching a glimpse of my soul kept me alive, realizing I was *more than* my mind and my will, because when those things are gone, the soul is still available."

I have come to believe that our soul is the most essential, precious thing about any of us. And, paradoxically, our soul is something we are the least aware of, the least concerned about, until our lives begin to fall apart. I have come to believe that our souls help to save us—not in and by themselves, but because their needs can drive us to God who alone can save us, and to the things only God can provide.

But I also believe that for many people the soul is neglected. The key to our happiness, our well-being, our joy, our sense of meaning and purpose, is our embodied soul. But the last thing we suspect when we struggle is that the problem is in our soul. This is because we have been trained to think of ourselves not as having a *soul*, but as being a *self*.

The world in which we live is constantly bombarding us with messages that we, and everyone around us, is a self, and it is the leading cause of our lack of well-being, our strife in our relation-

> How would you describe the difference between having a soul and being a self?

ships, and for many, it is the root of our self-hatred. Fortunately our soul, like the author said on the podcast, "is a wild creature that knows how to survive." My hope for this book is that your soul will be able to stop trying to survive and will learn how to *thrive*.

FALSE NARRATIVE: YOU ARE A SELF

When it comes to forming our sense of identity, we begin not with our spiritual dimension but with our bodily dimension. And we begin not with our sense of connection, but of isolation. "I am a self" is the dominant identity narrative. The twentieth century has been called "the century of the self." The self, not the soul, emerged as the central defining term of who we are, and the result has not been positive.

A few years ago, the *Journal of the American Medical Association* cited a study that indicated that in the last one hundred years "the people who lived in each generation were three times more likely to experience depression than folks in the generation before them." All this, despite the rise of the mental health profession. James Hillman, renowned psychologist, gave this provocative title to his 1993 book: *We've Had a Hundred Years of Psychotherapy—And the World's Getting Worse.*

This is in no way a denigration of psychotherapy and counseling. I have benefited greatly from therapy, and I encourage everyone I know to receive counseling. Despite the fact that the word *psychology* literally means "the study of the soul" (the Greek word for the soul is *psychos*), the soul, or spiritual dimension, of the human person has largely been removed in much of modern psychology. However, therapists and psychologists who operate from a Christian worldview include the soul as an important part of counseling and therapy. Without the soul, the human person is reduced to a *self*. The dominant narrative in our world today is that we are selves, not embodied souls.

The self is a construct that is built on the narrative that says you are an accidental, carbon-based life form that is here today and gone tomorrow. The self is an isolated individual. As such, the self is primarily interested in survival and finds its value in how it looks, what it possesses, and what others say about it. The self thrives on the currencies of money, sex, and power, on résumés, branding, accomplishments, notoriety, physical appearance, and entertainment. The self is built on *self*-reliance: "Look out for your*self*," "Take care of your*self*." In this sense, the self becomes an idol—everything revolves around the self.

The self can be easily misled into trusting in non-reality. Misled into thinking beauty, goodness, and truth are subjective and that money, fame, or success will make us happy. The self is taught to believe that perception is reality, and that what matters is what people think about us. The self consists of the accumulated ideas and images it has of itself, and the ideas and images it wants to project to others in order to find acceptance and affirmation. In short, *the self is too small to bear the weight of who we really are.* Only the soul can do that, because our souls are real, eternal, and massive. And our souls have built into them the way to wellness. We just have to listen to them.

TRUE NARRATIVE: YOU HAVE A SOUL

When we focus on our self, our sacred soul is neglected. Our soul has a completely different value system. It knows what really matters and what does not. Our soul cares for vastly different things than what our self cares for. Our soul cares about harmony, connection, and integration. Our soul is all about integrity—about what is real, true, beautiful, and good. Our soul wants to be desired for itself, longs to be loved without condition, and yearns for connection with deeper realities—spiritual realities. Our soul hungers for God (Psalm 42:1). The soul knows there is a God—and longs to live in surrender to God.

What is your soul? Your embodied soul is your *founding life form*. The Latin word for soul is *animus*, where the word "animate" comes from. Your soul animates your life; your soul gives life to your body. Your soul is the wellspring of your spiritual emergence from birth to death. Your soul is a non-physical substance, but it is very real.

God breathed your soul into you. "And the LORD God formed man of the dust of the ground, and breathed into his nostrils the breath of life; and man became a living *soul*" (Genesis 2:7 KJV, emphasis added). Your soul is a gift. It can be neglected to your peril, or it can be nurtured and nourished to your salvation. Your soul can be saved, but it can also be lost: "For what is a man profited, if he shall gain the whole world, and lose his own soul?" (Matthew 16:26 KJV). As John Ortberg points out, "[Your soul] weighs nothing but means everything." And yet our soul is something we seldom think about.

Rarely do we find good teaching about our souls, not even in our churches. Ironically, I find more "soul talk" going on *outside* of the church. Taylor Momsen, a child star and television actress, had some friends die from suicide and accidents, and she suffered from depression and substance abuse. She said she turned to music to heal her. She said, "I had given up on life, but then I turned to music. Rock and roll is food for the soul." How can rock music be "food for the soul"? I suspect she felt something deeply in music, and *soul* is the only word she could find to speak about this kind of depth.

We are more likely to hear the word *soul* in terms of music (e.g., soul music) than we do in our churches. These popular songs all contain the word *soul* in their titles:

- "Heart and Soul" by Huey Lewis & the News
- "All That You Have Is Your Soul" by Tracy Chapman
- "Satisfy My Soul" by Bob Marley & The Wailers
- "Soul Man" by Sam & Dave
- "Show Me Your Soul" by Red Hot Chili Peppers
- "Soul Survivor" by the Rolling Stones
- "Who Will Save Your Soul" by Jewel
- "Beautiful Soul" by Jesse McCartney

Soul is a word we see all over culture—though without much spiritual meaning. There is soul food, soul friendship, soul brothers and soul sisters, and soulmates. This is because we know, instinctively, that there is something deeper than we can name. The word *soul* is often used but seldom understood.

Your soul is the most real part of you. As Ruth Haley Barton writes, your embodied soul "is the 'you' that exists beyond any role that you play, any job that you perform, any relationship that seems to define you, or any notoriety or success you may have achieved. It is the part of you that longs for more of God than you have right now." Our souls seek harmony, want to share deeply with one another, and yearn to be free from practices that harm; and our souls long for integrity—to show on the outside who they are on the inside.

> Do you agree the word *soul* is often used but seldom understood? How often do you hear teaching on the soul or conversation around things of the soul?

WHERE DOES YOUR SOUL COME FROM?

Your soul was created by God and breathed into your body (Genesis 2:7). It was made by God: "Before I formed you in the womb I knew you" (Jeremiah 1:5). You were intended before the foundation of the world (Ephesians 1:4). Your soul is the essence of who you most deeply are. The Trinity is the Creator of your embodied soul, created in the image of God (Genesis 1:26-27). It is the bridge between your essence in God and your existence in the world. Your soul is your deepest nobility, what makes you sacred and precious and valuable.

The soul can be difficult to define. The great theologian Karl Barth confessed, "We shall search the Old and New Testaments in vain for a theory of the relation between the soul and body." Your soul is a mystery—a beautiful, powerful, wonderful, mysterious part of you. It cannot be weighed on a scale. But your soul is constantly at work in your life. Theologian Ray Anderson said, "The soul is the 'whole person' existing in a bodily form and state." Anderson says it well: the soul exists in a bodily form. Christianity does not teach *dualism*— the notion that our souls and bodies are separate. This was the teaching of the Greek philosophers, and it has found its way into the minds of many Christians. We are, and always will be, ensouled bodies, or embodied souls.

Your embodied soul is a gift from God that requires care. Your soul needs, actually demands, care. This was my own experience, and I found out the hard way. When I finally had the courage to face my lack of joy, my own loss of purpose and meaning, I assumed it was because I had not been more diligent in my Christian life. I have come to believe that many emotions, such as a lack of joy, are like indicator lights in our car that tell us when something is wrong. The problem for me was a downcast soul:

> Why are you cast down, O my soul,
>> and why are you disquieted within me? (Psalm 43:5)

How do our souls become cast down? When their needs are not met or when they endure a hardship. Our souls, though powerful and eternal, are actually very needy. And this can be a good thing. Our souls refuse to be neglected, and if we listen to their needs we will tend to them. And like the psalmist we will discover that the needs of our souls are met only in God:

> Hope in God; for I shall again praise him,
>   my help and my God. (Psalm 43:5)

TEN THINGS YOUR SOUL CAN'T ENDURE

Our souls are powerful and eternal, but there are a lot of things they cannot endure. In fact, there are at least ten things the soul cannot endure:

1. Harm to our bodies
2. Feeling unwanted
3. Guilt
4. Shame
5. Disconnection from God
6. Boredom
7. Sin
8. Being victimized
9. Meaninglessness
10. Nonexistence

Let me unpack these things.

Our souls are one with our bodies, and when our bodies are harmed or mistreated, our souls hurt as well. Both pleasure and pain—originating in our bodies—are felt in our souls. When someone hurts our bodies (abuse), our souls are fractured—and if it's severe, they are broken (though not beyond healing).

Our souls cannot endure feeling unwanted and unwelcome. Have you ever walked into a social setting and sensed that you were not welcome, that people did not want you to be there? That pain you felt is a soul pain. After all, your soul was created to be lovingly accepted by God and others.

Our souls also cannot endure guilt and shame. Shame is different from guilt. We feel shame for who we are, but we feel guilt for what we have done. Guilt can be a good thing—if we have done

> Journal about a time when you experienced one of these ten things that the soul cannot endure. How do you think this affected your soul?

something wrong, we should feel bad about it and want to repent and correct it. Our souls are what want to find forgiveness and make amends.

Our souls cannot stand deadness and boredom. This is not simply enduring standing in a long line at the DMV or being on hold on the phone with music looping while we wait for the customer representative. The deadness and boredom I am talking about comes from the lack of being a part of something exciting, meaningful, purposeful, and adventurous. Our souls long for this, and if we cannot get it we will settle for an amusement park or marathon-watching TV. But our souls are spiritual in nature, and find the secular to be dull. The soul is made to soar in transcendence.

Our souls also cannot endure sin. Sin always hurts us. Some sin may be pleasurable for a time (otherwise no one would sin) but our souls know what sin is—namely, that which destroys us. God is not against sin because God is prudish; God is against sin because it hurts us. So he designed our souls to recoil at it—sooner or later.

Our souls also hate being victimized. If someone has harmed us, that pain can become a part of our story. Our souls want to walk into our story and own it, not be controlled by it.

Finally, our souls also hate meaninglessness and nonexistence. They cannot stand spending energy on things that do not matter, on living a life that doesn't mean anything. And our embodied souls cannot endure the notion of dying and no longer existing. The fear of death, not just of our own but of those whom we love, is a deep fear in our souls.

TEN THINGS YOUR SOUL NEEDS

You have a mind that is phenomenal. It can think and reason and calculate; it can imagine and dream and envision. You have a body that is amazing. It is made of over thirty trillion cells, all working miraculously, without much help from you. Your heart and lungs and liver are all doing their thing right now, even as you read. You have a will, a power to decide and to act and plan and execute and accomplish. Your soul is interacting with all of these dimensions of who you are.

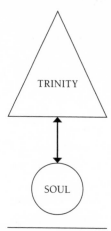

Figure 1.1. The Trinity fulfills the desires of the soul

But your soul is more than an operating system; it came factory loaded with a lot of needs. Your embodied soul is durable and tough, but very needy. Your soul was intricately designed with several needs; there is no debating them or escaping them—they simply must be met. God, the Father, Son, and Holy Spirit, created your soul with each of these relational needs that only the Trinity can fulfill. And because God is good, all that we need God has provided as free gifts. Fulfilling these desires is an act of grace.

There are at least ten God-created longings of the soul:

1. To see my body as sacred
2. To be wanted, desired
3. To be loved without condition
4. To be intimately connected to God
5. To be forgiven forever
6. To be alive and empowered to adventure
7. To be holy, virtuous
8. To own my story

9. To be called to a life of purpose

10. To be glorified and live forever

First, our souls, which are embodied, long for our body to be regarded as sacred. Harm to our bodies is harmful to our souls, because they are united.

Second, our souls long to be wanted. When you feel welcome, when you feel as if other people really desire you and are glad you are there, your soul feels joy and peace.

Third, our souls also want to be loved, not for anything we do, but for who we are. We all know when people are showing affection or appreciation for what we have done. The soul's longing to be loved is to be loved for absolutely no reason.

Fourth, our souls long for God. And we connect to God, to the spiritual realm, in so many ways, not just in church. A piece of art, a wildflower, a calming or exhilarating song, connect to our souls.

Fifth, our souls long for forgiveness. Just as our souls cannot endure being unforgiven, our souls rejoice when we have found real forgiveness. When the wrong we have done has been acquitted, our souls find release.

Sixth, our souls also long to be fully alive. They long for an adventure. Our souls want to be a part of something thrilling.

Seventh, just as our souls reject sin, they also long for holiness. Our souls have been preprogrammed for purity. They long to be clean. When I walk in holiness—when I do the next thing I know to be right—my soul feels whole. I am living into who I was designed to be.

Eighth, our souls come into this world in a time, a place, a family, and a culture. Our lives become our story. And our souls long for our story to have meaning. We want our lives—with their pains and losses, as well as joys and successes—to matter.

Ninth, our souls also long to live a life that makes the world a better place. For most of us, we long to feel like we are called to something, to be a part of something. We are born with a set of gifts, with a specific temperament, and certain talents and passions that come together to form our unique calling.

Tenth and finally, we long for glory. Not merely the fame and glory that come in this life, but to be glorified in the next. Our souls long for eternal life. Every one of these longings has been met in God and by God. There is nothing we have to do to earn that fulfillment—they are all a gift.

> To what extent have you experienced any of these ten longings of the soul?

CHRIST IS THE WAY TO WELLNESS OF SOUL

Our souls, while eternal and enduring, cannot endure deadness and boredom, rejection and sin. And our souls are very, very needy. In fact, the needs of our souls are far greater than what this world can give. As John Ortberg writes, "The soul's infinite capacity to desire is the mirror image of God's infinite capacity to give. . . . The unlimited need of the soul matches the unlimited grace of God." The good news is that the God who created our needy souls has, by grace, provided all that our souls will ever need. We cannot achieve or attain these things our souls need. They have to be given to us by God, as a gift. And God has provided all of those things in Jesus.

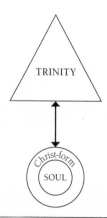

Figure 1.2. **When we come into faith in Christ, the Christ-form surrounds our soul**

1. In Christ I am a sacred member of Jesus' body.

2. In Christ I am wanted.

3. In Christ I am loved.

4. In Christ I am connected to God.

5. In Christ I am forgiven.

6. In Christ I am alive and empowered to adventure.

7. In Christ I am holy.

8. In Christ I am the owner of my story.

9. In Christ I am called.

10. In Christ I am hidden and glorified.

If we seek true and complete fulfillment from the things of this world we will search in vain. People may want us, or they may not.

The soul cannot endure . . .	The longings of the soul . . .	In Christ . . .
Harm to our bodies	To see my body as sacred	I am a sacred member of Jesus' body.
Feeling unwanted	To be wanted and desired	I am wanted.
Shame	To be loved without condition	I am loved.
Disconnection with God	To be intimately connected with God	I am connected to God.
Guilt	To be forgiven forever	I am forgiven.
Boredom	To be made alive and to take part in an adventure	I am alive and empowered to adventure.
Sin	To be holy and virtuous	I am holy.
Victimization	To own my story	I am the owner of my story.
Meaninglessness	To be called to a life of purpose	I am called.
Nonexistence	To be glorified and live forever	I am hidden and glorified.

Figure 1.3. The wellness of the soul

People may love us, or they may not. To fulfill the deep needs of our soul, we must look to Jesus. When we come into faith in Christ, when we are born from above and enter into the kingdom of God, our lives become "hidden with Christ" (Colossians 3:3). In this sense, the "Christ-form" surrounds our soul, as seen in figure 1.2. In Christ alone we find what our souls are looking for. In Jesus alone we find wellness for our souls.

In Christ I discover that I am desired. In Christ I learn that I am loved. By the work of Jesus on the cross, I find that I am forgiven forever. And through Jesus' resurrection, I realize that I am risen with him. By the work of Jesus I have been made holy; by his victory over sin and death, I discover that I am free. In Christ I learn that I have been gifted and called.

"All I have needed thy hand hath provided," as the hymn says. God's amazing grace has saved a wretch like me. "My sin—oh, the bliss of this glorious thought! / My sin—not in part but the whole / Is nailed to His cross and I bear it no more; / Praise the Lord, praise the Lord, oh my soul."

The rest of this book will examine how God, in Christ, has created the good and beautiful you and has provided for the deepest needs of your soul. Each chapter will examine these actions of God on your behalf and my behalf.

IT IS WELL WITH MY SOUL

The week of intensive counseling was the beginning of my soul restoration. During that week I stopped and acknowledged that I *had* a soul, something I had forgotten and neglected. Indeed, I am a soul, and to neglect my soul is to neglect my entire person. But that week was only the beginning of the work I needed to do to develop wellness in my soul. The primary change in me was learning to live again with my soul in mind in all that I do. I was able to see that success is something to be thankful for but not to rely on, and in fact is something to be careful about. We simply must guard our souls.

Over the next few years I would relearn to love the things my soul loves: loving God, first and foremost; loving that I am desired and loved by God; loving being made alive in Christ; loving being forgiven forever by the cross and living with no condemnation; loving the unique calling God has given me; and loving the reality that I, and those I love, will one day rule and reign and dance and sing in the new heaven and the new earth. And in the meantime, taking successes lightly.

A few years after my own healing journey, I had dinner with Richard Foster. I shared with him my own story of soul restoration. "Way back when, you told me my life would change, and that I must guard my soul. How did you know this would happen?" I asked.

"Because it happened to me. That is why I tried to warn you."

"Well," I said, "I wish I would have listened."

"You listened as best you could," Richard said. "There are many things we just have to go through on our own to fully understand."

One of the odd things people who have done counseling, or been through therapy, or through twelve-step programs, will often say is, "I am actually grateful for my struggle." One friend of mine even said, "My addiction saved my life." I used to think that was crazy. Now I know it is absolutely true.

> Think about a time you struggled. Can you say you are grateful for that struggle? Take some time to write down things you can be grateful about in that struggle.

I am sad for the few years I struggled as my soul atrophied, but I am not sad that I struggled. It led me to a new kind of love and freedom and passion I could never have experienced if I had not struggled. I am so grateful to be able to say, "It is well with my soul."

Holy Leisure

Dolce far niente—"the sweetness of doing nothing."

One of the most powerful soul-training exercises I have ever done is a practice called *holy leisure*. In simple terms, holy leisure is "doing nothing, for God's sake." It is important to get the emphasis on the right clause: we do nothing, but we do it for God. Richard Foster writes about this in his classic book, *Celebration of Discipline:*

> The church Fathers often spoke of Otium Sanctum, "holy leisure." It refers to a sense of balance in the life, an ability to be at peace through the activities of the day, an ability to rest and take time to enjoy beauty, an ability to pace ourselves. With our tendency to define people in terms of what they produce, we would do well to cultivate "holy leisure" with a determination that is ruthless to our datebooks.

I can think of no practice that is more needed for our frantic, fast-paced, over-scheduled world than holy leisure, for the reasons Richard describes.

The central tenet of this book is that we are created by God with everything we need, everything our souls long for, and that we do not have to strive to meet these needs. God fulfills these needs as gifts to us. But everything within us wants to control, to push, to earn, and to achieve. Holy leisure puts this desire to death like nothing else I have done. In a sense, it is the simplest of all practices: just . . . do . . . nothing. In another sense, it is the most challenging practice we can engage in. This is due in part to the fact that our world calls this "killing time," which makes us feel false guilt when we do so. Nothing could be further from the truth. Holy leisure is "investing time" in resting in God.

When we created *The Spiritual Formation Workbook* for Renovaré, I put holy leisure as one of many prescribed practices, which included other disciplines such as Bible reading, worship, prayer, and fellowship, to name a few. When Dallas Willard saw the list of practices, he pointed at holy leisure and said, "This will be the one people will find the most difficult."

I said, "Surely not! I mean, doing nothing—what could be easier than that?"

Dallas was right. In every group in which I field-tested this list of practices, holy leisure was the one that people routinely said, "Yeah . . . I didn't end up doing this one."

Why was it so difficult? Because doing nothing is not something we ever do intentionally. To be sure, we all waste time now and again. But to set aside time to do it—that is foreign to us. It just feels strange. And it stirs up something within us that wants to do, to accomplish, to make the most of our . . . time.

The reason for beginning with this practice is to help us embed these narratives: life is a gift; we are a gift; we did not create ourselves or earn God's love and forgiveness; we did not merit new life in Christ; and our future life in glory is not something we earn. We did nothing to receive these gifts. Practicing holy leisure is a way to live into this reality. To embrace simply *being* instead of *doing* is difficult for most of us. This practice, if we can endure it, will bring peace into our souls.

So how do you practice holy leisure?

- Set aside a set amount of time in your schedule.
- Start with five or ten minutes doing nothing. You may find that you can spend longer than five to ten, and if so you may want to

try thirty or forty-five minutes—though this will be difficult for many, especially the first time if you have never done it.

- Find a comfortable place to sit still for this time period.
- Do *not* do anything that *accomplishes something.*
- Just be. Do not do.

Through the years I have done this practice in groups, and there are some common questions people ask. I will address some of the main ones:

1. Can I read my Bible during this time?

   Answer: No. But if you feel a strong need to look up a passage, feel free to do so. Just be sure you are not reading as a means of preparing for some future task, such as a Bible study or sermon. Remember: you are not to *accomplish* anything.

2. Can I write in my journal during this time?

   Answer: Maybe. If you are hit with an insight that you want to write down, feel free to write in a notebook or journal. But as with the Bible, be sure you are not using this time to *do* something. Your goal is to do *nothing.*

3. Can I take a walk during this time?

   Answer: Maybe. Once again, it is all about your motive. If you are secretly trying to get in some exercise, then the answer is no. That would be accomplishing something. But if you find yourself outside and want to walk to a lovely spot, feel free to do so.

The point of this practice is to become comfortable doing nothing, which puts to death our need to establish our worth through what we accomplish. If we make this practice a part of the rhythm of our lives, we will discover the joy of unhurried living, as well as the blessing of knowing that all of life is grace.

In my experience, many people will find this *very* difficult, and for some, even unpleasant. Many people have even said to me, "When I tried holy leisure it was a disaster—an epic fail!" If that is the case for you, do not be discouraged. The rule of thumb for all soul-training exercises is this: do as you can, not as you can't. Simply do this exercise for as long as you are able, and be at peace. Few people do it well the first time, so give yourself a lot of grace. Focus on *being* and not *doing* for as long as you are able, and count on it being easier the more you practice it.

two

you Have a sacred Body

One of my favorite moments in my church, Chapel Hill UMC, is when we have a baptism. My pastor and colleague in ministry, Jeff Gannon, is a maestro of the sacraments. He loves offering Communion and performing baptisms—especially baptisms. As Methodists, we baptize both infants and adults, and we do it by pouring water on the head of the person being baptized. Jeff does not merely *sprinkle* water on the baptismal candidates; he *splashes* water all over them. We must have towels ready. This is because Jeff understands the importance of the body and of physical matter as sacraments—the physical as spiritual and sacred. My favorite part of the baptisms is the sacrament of *chrismation*. Chrismation is an ancient Christian practice in which the minister or priest anoints the recipient with oil, making the sign of the cross on the forehead, eyes, lips, ears, chest, hands, and feet, each time saying, "The seal of the gift of the Holy Spirit."

As Jeff anoints the infant's forehead, he says, "I anoint you in the name of the Father, the Son, and the Holy Spirit, and I mark you with the sign of the cross that you might know that you belong to Jesus."

He then anoints their hands and feet, saying, "I bless your hands that you will always serve him, and your feet that you may always follow him." Then he anoints their heart, saying, "We bless your heart that you will always know how deeply he loves you." Next he anoints their lips, saying, "We bless your lips that you will always speak of love for him." Finally, he anoints the top of their head: "We pray the blessing of Jesus on the whole of your life, that you will know he is the friend who will never leave you or abandon you."

Our congregation loves this practice so much that when parents bring their child forward for baptism and chrismation, they take off the child's shoes so that their bare feet can be directly anointed. The people love it and expect Jeff to do it. I suspect this is because our souls, which are embodied, instinctively know that our bodies are sacred and that they are meant to be given to God. Even the oil he uses smells heavenly. Jeff told me that even adults insist on chrismation as a part of their baptism. Recently an adult woman came forward for her baptism with bare feet so he could bless them. Afterward she said, "I am going to smell the goodness of God for the rest of the day!"

I am moved to tears during chrismation, especially when it is for a little child. Their little bodies, fearfully and wonderfully made, have been designed for a glorious, good, and beautiful life. Will these wonderful bodies be used for the glory of God? That is what we hope and pray.

In these moments during chrismation, I am reminded of the sacred nature of our bodies. It is something I should see all of the time, but fail to see. We live in a world in which *bodies are commodities*, things to be used, evaluated, and judged as purely physical. Even in the Christian world, we have not properly valued our bodies, at best, and have at times been guilty of seeing the body as something to be despised. More often than not, I have found we live with the false narrative that our bodies have nothing to do with our spiritual lives.

FALSE NARRATIVE: MY BODY HAS NOTHING TO DO WITH MY SPIRITUAL LIFE

A dominant narrative—even if only implicit—is that our bodies have nothing to do with our spiritual lives. Except, perhaps, to get in the way. Whether we are aware of it or not, we live with a *dualistic* view of the human person: we are spirits who have bodies. Our spirits are *good* and our bodies are *bad*, so the narrative goes. This narrative, that the body is an impediment, goes all the way back to the Greek philosophers, in particular to Plato. Plato believed the body was a kind of "prison for the soul" and gladly longed for the soul's release from the body. The false narrative is that our souls are pure and good and holy, but our bodies are sullied and sinful.

Most of the people I know, including myself, see the body as a *commodity*. We see it as a physical entity, and we evaluate it on the basis of its appearance, size, strength, or ability. The gorgeous, the overweight, the muscular, or the skilled are what we focus on instead of the person behind those physical traits, because we are trained to see the physical first. Many of us spend our lives feeling bad about our bodies. They are too tall, too short, too fat, or too thin; they are misshapen or wrinkled or blemished. And many of us spend a great deal of time and money and energy trying to get our bodies to *look* better or *perform* better.

Have you personally wrestled with this narrative about the body, that it is disconnected from our soul or that it gets in the way of our spiritual life?

In short, the dominant narrative about our bodies is that they have nothing to do with our spiritual lives except hinder us in our spiritual formation. In truth, our bodies are an essential and indispensable aspect of our spiritual formation. Everything we do in the spiritual life (pray, love, serve, study, worship) involves our bodies. Yet there is very little teaching in our churches about the role and significance and sacredness of our bodies in spiritual formation. The body is seen as a source of sin, or shame, or an obstacle to growth. Seeing our bodies—our good and beautiful bodies—as *sacred* instruments is essential if we are to live a vibrant life and have wellness in our embodied soul.

TRUE NARRATIVE: I HAVE A SACRED BODY

It is surprising that Christians have had trouble viewing the body as sacred. When God created Adam and Eve in physical bodies, he declared these embodied people as "very good" (Genesis 1:31). Even more than this, our entire faith is built on the incarnation—the belief that God became human and took on a body in the form of Jesus of Nazareth. Jesus had a body, *corpus Christi*, and we know instinctively that his body was and is sacred. But we must remember that Jesus came as an infant. He had a body exactly like ours, though he never sinned. Perhaps that is why theologian Ray Anderson believes our anthropology, how we understand the human person, should begin with Jesus and not Adam. If we start with Adam, we are likely to start with the fall, which may explain why we have such low views of the body.

> Your body is sacred and it is the location of your person. Is this a new thought to you? What do you think of when you read this true narrative about the body?

Your body is sacred. It is the location of your person. If I want to interact with you, I must do it via your body—even if it is over a Zoom call. In fact, the challenge many of us had during the coronavirus pandemic was the loss of connection to real bodies; pixels and speakers are no replacement for actual bodies and live voices. The miracle that is you is and will always be embodied. God's design for the human person is to be embodied. God loves matter—God made a lot of it. And God loves human bodies—God made a lot of them. There are over seven billion of them living on this planet right now. They come in all shapes and sizes and skin colors.

Your body is not a commodity. It is not something to be used or abused. And it is certainly not irrelevant in your spiritual life. It is a sacred, intricately designed organism that is an inextricable part of you. I will never be able to find *you* anywhere other than in your body.

To be sure, our bodies are sacred in the eyes of God. Our bodies are deeply connected to our souls, making us one. In order to see this, we need to start by looking at the relationship between the body and the soul.

BODY AND SOUL

It was Saint Thomas Aquinas who coined the Latin phrase *anima forma corporis,* which means "the soul is the form of the body." The soul, as I said previously, is defined as the first principle of life for all humankind. *Anima* (the Latin word for "soul") animates that which is alive. We are a soul and at the same time a body. We must avoid dualism; human beings are a unity. The soul is in the body, and the body is in the soul. Put simply, we do not *have* souls—we *are* souls; we do not *have* bodies—we *are* bodies. And they are united. Our body needs our soul in order to live and move—to *animate* it. And our soul needs our body in order to reveal itself, to be made known, and to act. In this sense, the body is the instrument of the soul. They need each other. Together, they make us who we are. As Jennifer M. Rosner points out, "The body is not an accidental feature of our humanity; rather, our bodies fundamentally constitute what it means to be human."

> Take a few minutes to write down "the soul is the form of the body" in your journal. Reflect on the phrase, then write down what it means to you.

You—body and soul—are one of the most amazing beings on this planet. As Annie Grace states, "Your mind can do more than any computer. In fact, it creates computers. Your body is self-regulating, self-healing, and self-aware. It alerts you to the tiniest problems and is programmed to protect you, ensuring your survival. It is infinitely more complex than the most intelligent technology. It is priceless." There is so much information contained in a single cell of your body that it would take volumes of books to write out all of that information.

Your body came into being "factory loaded" with an amazing set of capacities. Your body knows how to distinguish colors and tastes even before you encounter the color green or the taste of honey. Your body already knows how to breathe, to eat, to see, and to drive a car long before you know what a car is. It is within you. God designed your body this way. When the doctor taps your knee and you kick out your leg? Your body already knows this. When the love of your life kisses you and your whole body trembles—your body already knows this, long before it happens.

Our bodies are also capable of learning so much more knowledge, knowledge that will need to be *acquired*. Your body has the ability to drive a car when you are a child, but it is not able to do so yet; it is not capable of mastering a two-thousand-pound vehicle at high speeds. So you start with a tricycle, then a bicycle with training wheels, then a bike without training wheels; your body is learning. And one day it will be ready to drive a car. And one day down the road (pun intended), you will find yourself driving on a long stretch of road without even thinking. Your body will be driving the car practically without your mind or will.

SIN AND GRACE IN OUR BODIES

Your body is also equipped with many urges. When it needs food, you feel hungry; when it needs water, you feel thirsty. Once when hiking I realized that I had forgotten to bring a canteen. I realized this a few miles up the mountain on a hot day. Soon I was focused on only one thing: water. Thankfully a passerby offered me a precious drink; I would have paid him a hundred dollars for that drink. The water was delicious and sent a cascade of pleasure through my body.

The vital urges of the body are in place to keep us alive and well. But those urges can become obsessive—this happens when the body's urge overrides the will.

In our bodies we sometimes feel a compulsion to act in ways that are contrary to what our souls and minds and will want. This is how the apostle Paul explains it:

> But in fact it is no longer I that do it, but *sin that dwells within me*. . . . Now if I do what I do not want, it is no longer I that do it, but *sin that dwells within me*. So I find it to be a law that when I want to do what is good, evil lies close at hand. For I delight in the law of God in my inmost self, but I see in my members another law at war with the law of my mind, making me captive to the law of *sin that dwells in my members*. Wretched man that I am! Who will rescue me from this body of death? Thanks be to God through Jesus Christ our Lord! (Romans 7:17, 20-25, italics added)

Sin comes to dwell in our bodies. Our bodies are not to blame; the sin is. The person addicted to food or sex may try to blame their bodies, but their bodies are not to blame.

The word for this is *compulsion*. That is what Paul is describing in Romans 7. This is how desires can come to rule us. In short, sin becomes embedded in us, and we try in vain to shake it. But it can be broken, and Paul says so in the last verse: "Who will rescue me from this body of death? Thanks be to God through Jesus Christ our Lord." Grace, the power of God in our lives, can break the power of sin in our bodies.

This why Paul encouraged the Christians at Rome to

> no longer present your members [parts of your body] to sin as instruments of wickedness, but present yourselves to God as those who have been brought from death to life, and present your members to God as instruments of righteousness. For sin

will have no dominion over you, since you are not under law
but under grace. (Romans 6:13-14)

By grace, the power of God in our lives, we can begin to present our
bodies to God as instruments of righteousness. Jesus has not only
taken away the guilt of our sin, he has broken the power of sin. The
cross is ground zero for the war against sin, not destroying all sin but
defeating it, so we can walk in freedom. It is now our job, as those
who have been made alive in Christ, to retrain our bodies to become
instruments of goodness.

The body can become an enemy or an ally in our spiritual formation in Christlikeness. When properly cared for, rested, nurtured,
and connected to the deepest longings of the soul—the transcendent—
our bodies can become our allies. In order for that to happen, we
must learn how to have dominion over our bodies. Paul used the
metaphor of an athlete to illustrate how to treat our bodies:

Athletes exercise self-control in all things; they do it to receive
a perishable wreath, but we an imperishable one. So I do not
run aimlessly, nor do I box as though beating the air; but I punish my body and enslave it, so that after proclaiming to others
I myself should not be disqualified. (1 Corinthians 9:25-27)

Self-control is required of an athlete. Olympic athletes rise early
and train hard, and are careful about what they eat and how much
they sleep. They pay attention to stretching and weight training, because they know that optimum performance demands it.

The same applies to our spiritual lives. We have bodies—
that is God's arrangement for our lives—and they are wonderful and beautiful in their own ways. They are our bodies

> Think of someone who through self-control pays attention to an area of their life, whether physical, emotional, or spiritual. Do you witness this training paying off in their life?

given to us so that we can offer them to God. Again, Paul states it beautifully: "I appeal to you therefore, brothers and sisters, by the mercies of God, to present your bodies as a living sacrifice, holy and acceptable to God, which is your spiritual worship" (Romans 12:1).

Of course, living bodies do not want to be sacrificed. They tend to crawl off the altar! What Paul means is that we are to *present* our bodies to God, to say, in effect, "God, this body is yours. You have given it to me as a gift. And I want to offer it to you as a gift in return. I am wholly yours—not only in my mind and will and spirit, but also in my *body*." It is a form of spiritual worship, because our bodies are *sacred*. The Christian story illustrates this best out of all the world's religions.

FIVE SIGNS THAT OUR BODIES ARE SACRED

The Christian story, the story centered around the biblical witness and person of Jesus, is a strong affirmation of the value of the human body. There are five parts to the story that are clear signs that point to the sacred nature of the body. They are:

1. Creation
2. Incarnation
3. Church
4. Eucharist
5. Glorification

1. God created bodies—and it was good. The creation story in Genesis tells that when God created the physical universe, God deemed it as good, in fact, very good: "God saw everything that he had made, and indeed, it was very good" (Genesis 1:31). The Hebrew word *tov*, which we translate as "good," means more than simply good. *Tov*, according to Bible scholar Scot McKnight, means magnificent, perfect, wonderful. *Tov* is a perfect sunset, a glorious work of art, a magnificent athletic feat, and an act of sacrificial love. It is everything good and right and true and beautiful.

At the center of the creation story is the creation of humankind. Genesis says:

> So God created humankind in his image,
>> in the image of God he created them;
>> male and female he created them. (Genesis 1:27)

This verse occurs right before the "very good" of Genesis 1:31. Many Christians begin their theological anthropology at Genesis 3—the story of the fall. But this is a mistake. We must begin our understanding of the human person—including the human body—with Genesis 1. While the fall is an important part of the story, it is not where we begin. If we start with Genesis 3, we easily slip into the mistaken view that the body is evil. But before the fall, the body is, in fact, good. Very good. It is the very artwork of God. The fall does not eradicate it. The body is forever *tov*.

2. *The incarnation: God took on a body*. As a response to the fall, God became human. We refer to this as the doctrine of the incarnation. The Latin word, *carne*, means "flesh" or "meat." When we have chili con carne, we are having "chili with meat." The incarnation means "God with meat." God took on flesh; Jesus took on not only a soul and a spirit, but also a body. This must not be passed over too quickly: *God took on a body*. This was unheard of in the religions and philosophies of antiquity. The strongest affirmation of the importance of the body, of its sacred nature, is that God himself took one on. And Jesus was not a mere ghost; he did not "seem" to be human— he was fully human.

As such, Jesus experienced every bodily sensation we feel, except he did not sin. He hungered, thirsted, suffered, felt fear and sorrow, and he even aged. If scholars are correct in thinking he died around the

---

Think for a moment about the fact that Jesus in the flesh experienced aging, from infancy to young adulthood.

age of thirty, he must have experienced bodily decline. I like to think that Jesus noticed a wrinkle or a gray hair. Jesus suffered physically, and he also died *physically*. We are told that he had a body when he was resurrected—again, he was not a ghost. And that same body ascended. And that same body exists today. Jesus became a human in a body and remains so even today. This is an incredible affirmation of the body.

3. The church: the body of Christ. After Jesus rose from the dead and before he ascended into heaven, he told his followers to wait in Jerusalem for the Holy Spirit to empower them. They would form not just a community, not just a group; they would become members of his "body." The church is the body of Christ. When we join the church we become members of Jesus' body. And not merely members of Jesus' body, but members of one another: "So we, who are many, are one body in Christ, and individually we are members one of another" (Romans 12:5). This is not just a pretty sentiment; it is an actual reality.

The early church understood this. Being the *body of Christ* was ground for their unity despite their outer diversity. In Christ there is no longer Jew or Greek, male or female, slave or free; there is no caste system or financial stratum—we are all one in Christ. In Christ, people are no longer a source of opposition, or superiority, or inferiority, or exclusion. When I enter the church sanctuary each Sunday, I pause to remind myself that I am experiencing and participating in the body of Jesus of which I am a member, as are all the people I see.

4. Eucharist: this is my body. And when the church gathered, Jesus instructed them, they were to have a meal in remembrance of him. On the night in which he was betrayed, Jesus took bread, broke it, gave it to his disciples, and said, "'This is my body, which is given for you. Do this in remembrance of me.' And he did the same with the cup after supper, saying, 'This cup that is poured out for you is the new covenant in my blood'" (Luke 22:19-20). Paul tells the Corinthian Christ-followers, "For as often as you eat this bread and drink the cup, you proclaim the Lord's death until he comes" (1 Corinthians 11:26).

Every time a Christian takes Communion, also known as the Lord's Supper or the Eucharist (three names for the same sacrament), they are taking in the body and blood of Jesus. This is based on Jesus' words: "Those who eat my flesh and drink my blood abide in me, and I in them" (John 6:56). It is in Communion that the body of Christ becomes a part of us. And not only that, Communion *transforms* us into the body of Jesus. Saint Nicholas Cabasilas writes, "While natural food is changed into him who feeds on it . . . here it is entirely opposite. The Bread of Life himself changes those who feed on him and transforms and assimilates them into himself."

John Calvin famously noted that he believed this, but the change Communion works within us is a miracle too lofty to understand: "Now if anyone should ask me how this takes place, I shall not be ashamed to confess that it is a secret too lofty for either my mind to comprehend or my words to declare. And, to speak more plainly, I rather experience than understand it."

I like to think of it this way: when I eat a peanut butter sandwich, it loses its original state and is absorbed into me. The sandwich becomes a part of Jim. But when I take Communion, it is reversed: I become a part of Jesus. As Calvin said, it is too lofty for me to comprehend. But this I know and *feel*: when I partake of the Lord's Supper, I have a more tangible sense that "I am one in whom Christ dwells and delights."

> Next time you participate in Communion, think on the truth that you are one in whom Christ dwells and delights.

5. Glorification: the resurrection of the body. Finally, one of the greatest affirmations of the sacredness of the body is the Christian teaching that we will be resurrected with bodies. One of the affirmations we say in the Apostles' Creed is "We believe in the resurrection of the body."

This does not only mean Jesus' body, but our own as well. What do we mean by this? In short, it means that our actual bodies will somehow be reassembled and resurrected into all-new bodies. I find that many Christians assume our current bodies will be discarded and we will be given entirely new bodies of a completely different nature. In fact, I find many Christians whose beliefs about heaven are more Greek than Hebrew, more informed by cartoons and movies than by the Bible.

The New Testament is unequivocal in its teaching that we are and will always be embodied beings. We will never be ghost-like souls. The Christian teaching is that when we die, our souls become detached from our current bodies. Our current bodies will begin the natural process of decay and disintegration. "Ashes to ashes, dust to dust," as they say. However, although the body is detached from the soul, it is not separated from it. The body along with the soul awaits the final resurrection.

Christianity teaches us that our life after death will also be embodied. Our current bodies are perishable—we are all going to die—but we will be resurrected and will be given new bodies just as Jesus' resurrection was, and is and will forever be, *in a body*.

> For this perishable body must put on imperishability, and this mortal body must put on immortality. When this perishable body puts on imperishability, and this mortal body puts on immortality, then the saying that is written will be fulfilled: "Death has been swallowed up in victory." (1 Corinthians 15:53-54)

This is what is known as *glorification*, which is the subject of chapter eleven. Our current bodies will be delivered from all past sicknesses and will recover complete wholeness.

This does not mean we shall put on a different body. We shall each put on again our own body. But this new body will be reconstructed, reconstituted, and will have attained another mode of existence—one that will be free from the imperfections, weaknesses, corruptibility, and mortality that characterizes its present nature.

The new body we will receive, our resurrection body, will not live under the limitations and constraints of our present bodies. Our bodies and our souls will be perfectly united and will work in unison. They will not work against us, but will be our allies in godliness. These bodies will not be subject to illness or suffering or death. Our bodies will achieve their ultimate destiny: to be transformed and transfigured.

But one thing we must be sure of: we *will* have bodies. As Christians, we must purge our minds of the dualistic notion of a ghost-like existence. Jesus had a real body that was touched (as Thomas requested), that was hungry (he ate with his disciples on the beach), and that physically ascended into the heavens, defying gravity.

THE BODY AS THE BRIDGE TO TRANSCENDENCE

The original design and plan for the human body is to interact with the transcendent dimension and, more specifically, to connect us to God. We cannot engage in a relationship with God apart from our bodies. Writing in the fourth century, Macarius of Egypt wrote,

> For as God created the sky and the earth as a dwelling for man, so he also created man's body and soul as a fit dwelling for himself to dwell in and take pleasure in the body, having for a beautiful bride the beloved soul, made according to his image.

Notice that Macarius does not say God longs to dwell in our souls only. God "created man's *body* and soul" as a fitting place for God to dwell. And what's more, he says God "takes pleasure" in our bodies, bodies that are made according to God's own image.

All Christian spiritual formation practices—from prayer to worship to solitude—involve the body. Some are directed at the body more than others, such as fasting and vigils, where the appetites of the body for food and sleep are forgone for a time as a means of training the body, and thus, the soul. But even in prayer we see how the body is involved. Making the sign of the cross, kneeling, closing one's eyes, bowing one's head, raising one's arms, and even laying prostrate on the ground, are all postures of prayer in which the body's position reflects the inner condition of the soul. In traditions where incense is used, the smell alerts the mind, through the body, that our prayers are rising to God. You are indirectly aware of the spiritual dimension through the sensory realm. Through the senses you discover the sacredness of every person, every flower, every stone. Through your eyes and feet you discover that you stand on holy ground.

When our soul participates in divine peace, brought about by grace, it communicates this to our body. God's divine beauty, reflected in the soul, is transmitted to the body, which in turn becomes radiant. During a particularly moving Maundy Thursday service, I remember serving Communion and seeing a countenance I had never before seen on the faces of the people. Their bodies—particularly their faces—were glowing with the light of Christ. For many years the people who attended this service would speak of this night, this service, as a sacred space, a thin place where heaven seemed to touch the earth in a palpable way.

> When have you experienced divine peace in your body? Have you ever seen someone's countenance change because of divine peace brought about by grace?

Joel Clarkson, author of *Sensing God*, tells the story about feeling spiritually dry when he was in seminary and how he went home to Colorado to ask his mother for advice. While they were sitting outside among the pine trees, sipping coffee, his mother's advice came in this form. She pointed to the beautiful elements of creation and said, "Don't worry about feeling close to God. He's reaching out to you at this very moment in these elements. It's his gift to you. To the whole world." Clarkson concludes, "Before anything else is true, existence comes to us as a gift of God's grace."

Not only is our existence a gift of grace, so is the existence of pine trees and so is the existence of our bodily ability to apprehend them. Our bodies are bridges to transcendence. Those glorious moments when God through beauty reaches out to us and touches our souls, he does so through our bodies. If we did not have bodies, God could not reach us. God sings his love to you in birdsong. God smiles at you in maple trees. God charms you with the color green. He gave you eyes to see sunsets, ears to hear rainfall, a nose to smell a rose. God's massive love appears in the small fragments. God is loving you in these moments, even if you do not know it. And if you did not have a body, you never could.

RESPECT YOURSELF

I have noticed that, as Christians, we are not very good at loving and respecting and caring for our bodies. And we are seldom happy with our bodies. We want them to look more attractive, or be stronger or leaner. We also often see them as obstacles to our holiness. For many of us, women and men, our bodies are sources of shame and temptation. Many women, for example, feel guilt and shame when their bodies do not "bounce back" after pregnancy. And of course, aging is a cause of shame for both men and women, as we look in the mirror and see sagging and drooping, wrinkles and aging spots that remind us we are no longer young.

But an essential part of what makes you good and beautiful is your amazing body. It is constantly working to serve you; it *is*, in fact, you. Your body is the only one you will ever have. A way we glorify God is to treat our body as a sacred vessel of honor, to love and care for it as we would a great treasure. Not because we should, but because it is.

MOVE

In the award-winning film *Chariots of Fire*, Olympic runner Eric Liddell is discussing with his sister, a fellow missionary, whether or not to take time off from his mission work to run in the Olympics.

He tells her, "God made me fast. And when I run, I feel God's pleasure."

That line has always stuck with me: *When I run, I feel God's pleasure*. Now, I realize that not everyone finds pleasure in running, or in exercising in general, but I do believe that God made us with bodies and these bodies are *made to move*. Before I was a Christian I knew of the joy of physical movement, from playing football and basketball and baseball. But after I became a Christ-follower, I began to see how much God loves our bodies and how much joy our bodies are capable of when we see them not as commodities or as something to starve or exhaust to look more attractive, but as sacred organisms that are united with our souls.

Movement has been linked to our well-being in many ways, not just to our bodies but to our brains. In her book *The Joy of Movement*, Dr. Kelly McGonigal writes, "Physical activity influences many other brain chemicals, including those that give you energy, alleviate worry, and help you bond with others. It reduces inflammation in the brain, which over time can protect against depression, anxiety, and loneliness." But what I find even more fascinating is that during physical activity, our muscles secrete hormones into the bloodstream that make our brain more resilient to stress. Scientists have called them "hope molecules." In other words, when your body moves, it produces *hope*. Of the many great reasons to exercise (strengthen the heart and muscles, lower blood pressure and cholesterol) I find the ability to give us hope the most fascinating and alluring.

The soul-training exercise I am encouraging you to try is to *move* in whatever way you can. I recognize that for many reasons some people are limited in their mobility. And I realize that there are factors such as age and physical health that will limit the kinds of movement, and the amount of movement, that you might be able to do.

One of the things I try to do when I move is to concentrate on a part of my body. For example, when I am engaged in walking or swimming, biking or yoga, I try to pay attention to my feet or my legs and will give thanks for them. Or I will feel the air going in and out of my lungs and offer praise for both air and lungs. Perhaps you are only able to take a short walk. If so, I encourage you to do this with a focus on your body.

If possible, try to exercise outdoors. This is sometimes called *green exercise*. Studies have shown that within the first five minutes of outdoor exercise "people report major shifts in mood and outlook. . . . Taking a walk outdoors slows people's internal clocks, leading to the perception of time expanding."

Sometimes when I walk I combine movement with prayer. Spiritual formation author Adele Calhoun calls this practice "prayer walking." She writes, "Some people do their best praying while they are moving." She suggests we go outside and take a walk through our neighborhood, praying for the people who inhabit those places such as houses and churches and schools, or perhaps hospitals or places of business.

"Prayer walking," she writes, "is a way of saturating a particular place and people with prayer. This discipline draws us out of prayers that are limited to our immediate concerns and into a larger circle of

God's loving attention." When you come across a school, for example, try walking by it in the company of Jesus. Pray for the people who work there and those who attend there.

No matter what you are doing—jogging, kayaking, or playing tennis or pickleball—try to combine (1) an appreciation for your body, (2) awareness of your body, and (3) awareness of God—the One who perfectly designed your amazing body. Like Eric Liddell, see if you can feel God's pleasure in your movement.

three

YOU ARE DESIRED

Dawn grew up in a family in which she felt she had a fairly happy childhood. But in her adult years she struggled greatly with emotional, psychological, and physical maladies. She never felt a sense of well-being, and had an underlying sense that she did not belong in the world. During a therapy session, her counselor asked her if she knew the circumstances of her birth. Dawn assumed that there was nothing to learn, but her mother had a life-threatening illness and she was not sure how many opportunities she would have to ask her, so she went to visit her and asked if there was anything about her birth that she had not been told. Her mother burst into tears and told Dawn that she had conceived her out of wedlock, and that she walked around the house during her pregnancy wishing that she were not having a baby. Dawn then understood her deep lack of belonging and began to seek God for healing of this deep wound.

One morning as she washed her breakfast dishes she looked out at the grass in her yard. Then her eyes were drawn to a particular blade of grass. She realized that the particular blade of grass she noticed was created by God and was meant by God to be in the world in this very clump of grass in this very yard. God spoke deeply into Dawn's soul, letting her know that she, too, was created by God and meant to be in the world.

When Dawn discovered the circumstances of her birth, she discovered for the first time in her life that she was an accident; she was not planned. And she was not originally wanted. Her mother did not feel love for her while she was in the womb. We all have a deep longing to be loved, a desire to be desired, a need to be needed. It is deeply woven into our souls. The feeling of being unwanted is very painful. It sends a shiver into our souls. That is because *we desire to be desired.*

FALSE NARRATIVE: YOU ARE AN ACCIDENT

The Russian writer Leo Tolstoy describes a view (not his own view, because Tolstoy was a Christian) of the human person, based on a theory of reality he saw emerging in his day. It is a narrative that maintains that everything is secular (meaning there is no God and no spiritual dimension to life or to humans). In his book *A Confession*, Tolstoy named this view of the human being:

> You are an accidentally united little lump of something. That little lump ferments. The little lump calls that fermenting its "life." The lump will disintegrate and there will be an end of the fermenting and of all the questions.

Tolstoy was describing the emerging intellectual view in his day, a view that is widely accepted today in the modern world.

This narrative was articulated by the atheist author Richard Dawkins, who wrote, "The universe, at the bottom, has no design, no purpose, no evil, and no other good. Nothing but blind, pitiless indifference. DNA neither knows nor cares. DNA just is." Science writer and atheist Marshall Brain echoes this narrative in the area of our souls: "Your 'soul' is make-believe just like Santa. When the chemical reactions cease, you die. That's the end of it."

According to this narrative, the deep longing to be wanted, the yearning to be connected to something bigger, the need to believe you were intentionally designed and desired, is simply make-believe. Because, this view holds, you are a mere accident. All of us are little lumps of matter that do not matter. We "ferment" for a time, then "disintegrate." Tol-

> Does this false narrative sound familiar to you in today's world? What does it make you feel or think?

stoy wrote those prophetic words in 1880. Dallas Willard, commenting on this view, wrote in 1997, "There has been no advance beyond this position since Tolstoy's day."

The accepted view of the human person in academia today, in the universities, is that we are accidental beings who only exist because a female egg and a male sperm began the "fermenting" that became you and became me. This narrative arose because the spiritual realm, God, and the human soul are not detectable by scientific inquiry. If it cannot be measured and quantified, the secular narrative maintains, then it is not real. God, the soul, prayer, and the afterlife are human constructs, fantasies and wishes not based on reality. Reality, this narrative holds, is secular. And somehow this narrative became accepted as true. Religion is tolerated as an opiate to the people, as a way to help people cope. God and the church and its teachings are matters of faith, not knowledge.

And yet, as Tennyson wrote, "Thou madest man, he knows not why, he thinks he was not made to die." We may not be sure why we exist, but we do know we are not keen on dying or comfortable with the belief that our loved ones who have died were just chemical reactions who ceased reacting, fermentation that just stopped fermenting. We look at the created world and feel that there must be a Creator. We see order and elegance in the world, we feel a longing for beauty and goodness and truth and want it for ourselves and for others, and we are not satisfied with the idea that our existence is all "blind" and "pitiless."

Something rings untrue with this narrative. Surely we are more than "a collection of atoms destined to disperse." Something about this creates a sense of dissonance. The longing to believe that we and all of those we love are not mere accidents that live for a time and then cease to be is something that simply will not go away. Perhaps the narrative that we are divinely designed, intently pursued, and lavishly loved precious beings who are, in fact, *intended* will not go away because it is true.

TRUE NARRATIVE: YOU ARE WANTED BY GOD

The Bible tells us another narrative: the good and beautiful God *intentionally* created the good and beautiful you. You are of divine origin, you were planned, you are wanted, and you are perfectly, intricately designed by God and loved into existence. God created you in order to be with you because God loves you. God designed you with marvelous capacities to think and feel and create, to love and be loved, and an unquenchable longing for the transcendent, for beauty, goodness, and truth. You were created to connect with God and to glorify God with your one, precious life. God designed you to live a life of joy and to enjoy life with God forever.

> Reflect on this phrase:
> "God created you in order to be with you because God loves you."

I am not big on surprise parties, but one time my wife put together a birthday party for me, and I was not aware of it. Several old friends gathered together, without my knowing, at a restaurant. When I came into the room and saw everyone excited to see me, I felt a warmth in my soul and body I had seldom experienced. Those smiling faces and loving eyes looking at me touched me in a very deep place. I think this is because *we all want to be wanted*. This is not an example of selfishness or narcissism. We have a deep need to know that we are desired and valued by others, even if only a few others—our souls hunger for this. In this life, in this broken world full of hurt people, it may be difficult to find. The good news is that the One who created us wants and desires us more than we can ever know.

We are not accidents or little lumps of something. We are all original works of art. Our value is determined by the One who made us and by the inherent qualities that we possess. While all metaphors break down, I find the metaphor of the seed to be a great illustration of our true identity. Seeds contain life and form that remain invisible to us. They are an *actuality* that contains a *possibility*. They contain a blueprint for something far greater than what we can see merely by looking at the seed. Foxgloves are one of my favorite flowers, but if you only look at its seed you can never imagine what it becomes. It looks like a tiny speck of dirt, but within that seed is a glorious purple flower that makes my heart glad.

Seeds contain a *form*. The great spiritual scholar and writer Adrian van Kaam uses a term for God that I have grown to love: the *Divine Forming Mystery*. I love this description of God because God is clearly divine and clearly mysterious and clearly loves to form. Look at the universe; it is full of matter. And every single inch of matter has been formed, from the stars we see at night to the large star we see in the day, which we call the sun. There is intention and structure and purpose to every single form. Genesis 1 describes God as One who forms: earth and sky and water, birds and beasts, fauna and flora, planets and stars, and finally ... humans. God created—God formed—and said that all of that was good. And when he formed the humans, he called it all very good (Genesis 1:31).

Fr. Adrian coined another term I love, a term he used to describe all human persons. He said that God, the Divine Forming Mystery, created "divinely formed mysteries," which is us. We are not accidental—we were created with intent. We are not lumps of something but intricately formed, highly complex beings. The Bible teaches us that as human persons, you and I have been *preformed*. Long before we were born, we existed in the mind of God. God, therefore, foreknew us.

In Jeremiah, God says to us: "Before I formed you in the womb I knew you, /and before you were born I consecrated you" (Jeremiah 1:5). The apostle Paul echoes that same sentiment: "For those whom he *foreknew* he also *predestined* to be conformed to the image of his Son, in order that he might be the firstborn within a large family" (Romans 8:29, italics added). God foreknew you, and you have been predestined—determined in advance by divine decree—to emerge and to be made in the image of Christ. Like the seed that contains a form, you came into this world with many forms (soul, body, spirit) and one other uniquely human form: the Christ-form. Your destiny is to be *con*-formed, and *trans*-formed, into the image of Christ. Your essence preceded your existence, and your essence and existence are fascinating.

YOU ARE GOD'S POEM

God made you. God deliberately made you: "Let us make humankind in our image, according to our likeness" (Genesis 1:26). There was no hesitation—there was a complete declaration. God said, "Let us make _____ (fill in your name)." You were intended. You are far from an accident. Psalm 139:13-16 offers this narrative for how you came to be:

> For it was you who formed my inward parts;
>> you knit me together in my mother's womb. . . .
>> My frame was not hidden from you,
> when I was being made in secret. . . .
> Your eyes beheld my unformed substance.

God formed you. God knit you together. God saw your frame long before any sonogram technician did. God's eyes beheld you, and looked at you with eyes of love.

And God is a great artist. From the tiny atom to the massive Milky Way galaxy, God has yet to create anything less than a masterpiece. Paul told the Ephesian Christians, "For we are His workmanship, created in Christ Jesus for good works, which God prepared beforehand so that we would walk in them" (Ephesians 2:10 NASB). The word "workmanship" is *poiema* in Greek, and it is where we get the term *poem*. You are God's poem. God said, "Let there be you," and you came to be, and it was good—a very beautiful poem. A poet *forms* words into a poem. I love this metaphor because words by themselves have a simple meaning, but when you put words together (as I am doing right now) they interplay with one another to create something greater than the sum of the words.

A good poem creates an image no one has ever imagined before. A good poem creates a resonance and a spark in the reader, brings delight, creates a depth of feeling, and can make you laugh or cry or feel awe. A good poem creates joyful shivers, and is full of mystery and magic. And that is what you are, especially in the mind of God. This is what God feels when God sees you. And is what others who know you can feel, in some measure, depending on if they have eyes to see and ears to hear.

You were called by name and created for God's glory (Isaiah 43:7). God has a name for you that no one else knows, not even you, not yet. One day God will give you a white stone "with a new name written on the stone that no one knows except the one who receives it" (Revelation 2:17 ESV). Jesus made you, and Jesus is holding you together, right now, even as you read: "in him all things in heaven and on earth were created . . . and in him all things hold together" (Colossians 1:16-17). God said to Isaiah as he says to each of us, "I have inscribed you on the palms of my hands" (Isaiah 49:16).

You are not an accidental little lump of something. You are not unwanted or unplanned. You are a divinely designed, unceasing spiritual being with an eternal destiny in God's great universe, as Dallas Willard often said. You were known and wanted from the foundation of the world, and you have been built to last. You are designed to make your own *poems*, your own creations. Made in the Creator's image, you are called to create, and your creating will never cease. While the body you inhabit now will expire and start decomposing, *you* will not. You will be composing and recomposing, ruling and reigning in the heavens, for all eternity (Revelation 22:5). People often create a three- or five-year plan. I tell people, "You should create a ten-thousand-year plan. Because, as we sing, 'When we've been there ten thousand years . . .'"

THE SOUL FELT ITS WORTH

We all long to be desired. It is embedded in our souls. We will spend time and money trying to get other people to find us desirable. The pursuit of being desired by others is fraught with frustration and failure. People are fickle and their evaluations of us are unreliable, often saying more about them than about us. If we have enough "likes" or get enough praise, we can feel, for a moment, that we are wanted or desired. But that can all change in the next hour. Jesus understands this need we have, and Jesus is the true answer to our longing to be desired.

Jesus became a human just like us. His incarnation is the source of our validation. His save-and-rescue mission was an act of love driven by God's desire for us. He is like the shepherd who searches high and low for the lost sheep. You and I are that sheep. He will go to any length to find us. God sent Jesus because we are the apple of God's eye. You and I matter to God more than we can know. We are worth the incredible risk God took in becoming human, in submitting himself to suffering and death. Jesus endured the hurt and rejection and abandonment in order for us to know that we are the object of God's love.

I love the Christmas hymn "O Holy Night" by Adolphe Adams. My favorite verse is, "Long lay the world in sin and error pining, till he appeared and the soul felt its worth." The incarnation is proclaiming to you and me that we matter to God. We bear God's image. The fact Jesus became human affirms that all human lives matter, that we are all of inestimable worth. Even in the midst of our failings and faults and peculiarities, the you that is you, uniquely you, matters to God. You and I will never discover our true worth in the eyes of others—even those who love us the most in this life. It is only in the eyes of Jesus that we can discover our true worth.

YOU ARE AN ORIGINAL

Some homeowners in Sweden discovered a painting in their attic. It had been left by the previous homeowner, who had assumed the painting was not of any value. But the new homeowners suspected it might be an original painting by Vincent van Gogh. They brought it to Amsterdam's Van Gogh Museum in 1991, but the curators there deemed it inauthentic because it lacked Van Gogh's trademark signature. However, a few years later, art historians used new technologies to reexamine the painting. They could tell by examination that it followed the exact brushstrokes used by Van Gogh in his other paintings. Adding to their certainty, an 1888 letter from Vincent to his brother Theo described the painting in detail, and even mentioned the exact day he painted it. It is now on display in the museum.

What makes the painting so valuable? It is an original Van Gogh. If they had not authenticated that it was painted by Van Gogh, it would not be so valuable. You and I are original works of God. We were divinely designed and created by a masterful Artist. We are all *originals*, and this is why we are so desirable. Each of us carries within us our own originality. As our lives unfold, we begin to see more and more how uniquely each of us has been designed. God has a divine reverence for our radical originality. This is why it is so painful to God when we devalue ourselves.

> When we dismiss an artist's creation as worthless, we are in essence dismissing the artist's creative process and heart in that creation. Do you ever realize you are hurting God, the Artist, when you dismiss or devalue the good creation he made in making you?

Jesus longs for us to repent of the sin of finding our worth as defined by the world. Jesus died and rose to establish our new life, our true life, that has been hidden in him from the beginning. To be hidden in Christ (Colossians 3:3) is to be taken out of this world that has drugged our original selves with cheap satisfactions. To be hidden in Christ is to live in the penetrating light of his original life. Our originality, transformed in Christ, is the deepest originality we can live into. Discovering our original selves in the light of Jesus is far better than being lost in the masses trying to establish worth in what we have, how we look, or what we accomplish. Christ in me is the emergence of my original self that is from eternity in him.

I feel the pull to find my validation, my desirability, in the world I live in every day. But I have learned it can never be found there. And I have come to believe that attempting to establish my worth in this world is not only being unfaithful to God, but is actually being disloyal to myself.

Nonetheless, God is forever faithful to us, forever loyal to us. God is loyal to our spiritual identity that he created out of love. Before you existed, God loved you. It was the love of God that brought you into being. For our part, we can reject it and often do. In so doing, we are rejecting our unique selves that came into existence without our asking for it or deserving it.

What will you do with this gift, with the unique gift-that-you-are? God longs that your loyalty to your soul be as great as God's loyalty is to you. God does not force you to do so—you can reject your true worth and neglect your sacred value. God does not coerce you into saying yes to your soul. God instead waits for your answer with infinite compassion and gentleness and patience. How you answer will determine

> Are you saying yes to your soul as the unique, valuable gift of God's creation,
> or adopting the narrative of the world that establishes your worth apart from God?

whether you are living your one true life, or one constructed from the narratives of your world. If you fail to live into your true spiritual identity, into the gift-you-are, you will suffer a sickness of soul. Your soul cannot endure the constant striving to establish your worth in any way other than in God.

YOUR EXISTENCE IS YOUR VALIDATION

What is at stake in all of this? Does it matter if we know and believe that we are a divinely designed gift? What will be lost if we do not understand that we have a soul? What can be gained by an awareness that we have dazzling dimensions, preformed and predestined, that have and will shape the person we are and become? Why is it important to understand that we are not images of God, but are made in God's image?

A great deal, it turns out. The single answer is this: if this is true, *then we do not need to find our identity—our identity will find us.* Our identity is given by God; we do not have to search for significance. Significance has found us, and living then becomes a process of discovering and living into that significance.

We do not need to seek validation. Validation, as they say, is for parking tickets. Your existence is your validation. You are, as Mark Nepo writes, "an invaluable, irreplaceable seed in the ground of existence, each of us a small miracle waiting to blossom in the large miracle." But there are voices who will try to tell you that you are not enough—not smart enough, not beautiful enough, not talented enough. We live in a culture of rejection. The world around you will tell you that you cannot be loved, how you look is undesirable, and what you have is insufficient. Those voices, those assessments, are not telling the truth. The truth about you is this: you are a divinely designed gift.

To believe that we are divinely designed gifts should not lead us to narcissism but to doxology; it should not cause us to have pride, but should cause us to experience humility. We did nothing, after all, to merit or earn or deserve it. God chose to create each of us with aptitudes and talents, within a specific time and place and family, with incredible capacities to think and feel and imagine and dream. This should lead us to live with wonder, awe, and reverence for who we are, and for the One who made us. We are divinely designed sacred people who have been created by the Father, Son, and Holy Spirit. As such, we should pray, as Macrina Weiderkehr prayed so eloquently, "O God, help me to believe the truth about myself, no matter how beautiful."

When Jesus said we should not worry about our lives, he asked us to make a comparison between ourselves and grass: "Consider the lilies of the field. . . . Even Solomon in all his glory was not clothed like one of these. But if God so clothes the grass of the field, which is alive today and tomorrow is thrown into the oven, will he not much more clothe you—you of little faith?" (Matthew 6:28-30). If God does such a fantastic job adorning the flowers and the grasses of the earth, how much more can he adorn us? In Dawn's story at the beginning of this chapter, she was given an epiphany that a single blade of grass "was created by God and was meant by God to be in the world in this very clump of grass in this very yard."

I think Jesus was saying the same thing. God cares about every single flower, about every blade of grass. And yet, the flowers and grasses are, as they say, "here today and gone tomorrow." But you and I are unceasing spiritual beings, not accidental little lumps that are here today and gone tomorrow. How much more does God intentionally design and entirely sustain you and me. We are divinely designed, and deeply loved, unceasing spiritual beings with an eternal destiny in God's great universe. As such, we are a part of a larger and more significant divine conspiracy. You are a divine work of art, a masterpiece just as you are. But God is not done with you. God, "by the power at work within us is able to accomplish abundantly far more than all we can ask or imagine" (Ephesians 3:20).

I have found that remembering my Source, remembering that God, the Divine Forming Mystery, formed me and formed you, fills me with joy and passion. Remembering that our formation began before we were born, remembering that God lovingly preformed all people, and remembering that God is the hidden ground of all of our lives is

> Set your mind on this thought from above: that God, the Divine Forming Mystery, formed you.

a "thought from above" (Colossians 3:1-2) worth setting our minds on.

To that end, I have also found it useful to pray a prayer written by Fr. Adrian van Kaam. I leave it with you as a kind of benediction:

> Whisper to me again
> How you formed me in my mother's womb,
> Fashioned me over generations,
> Over eons of unfolding of the earth
> Until it could bear life
> On its flaky crust, the dust
> From which you formed our earthly frame
> Endowing each of us with a name
> Known to you alone.
> Remind me how I dwelt in you,
> My source and origin,
> A call from eternity,
> An archetype of life to be
> Unique and irreplaceably
> Your own.

Lectio Divina
Psalm 139 and Ephesians 2:10

A deep need in our souls is the desire to be desired. We want to be wanted. And we love being loved. Perhaps your parents excelled at showing you that you were—and are—wanted, that you were planned and desired. Or perhaps you did not get that message. Perhaps you were adopted or abused or came from a broken home, or, like the story of Dawn at the beginning of this chapter, your parents were not ready to be parents. No matter your situation, God wanted you. God planned for you long before you were conceived. And God desires you and desires to be with you every moment of your life.

For me, Psalm 139:13-16 has always been a glorious expression of God's desire for us, of God's intricate involvement in every aspect of our conception and development.

> For it was you who formed my inward parts;
>   you knit me together in my mother's womb.
> I praise you, for I am fearfully and wonderfully made.
>   Wonderful are your works;
> that I know very well.
>   My frame was not hidden from you,
> when I was being made in secret,
>   intricately woven in the depths of the earth.
> Your eyes beheld my unformed substance.

In your book were written
> all the days that were formed for me,
> when none of them as yet existed.

The other passage that speaks so powerfully about God's pre-planning for our lives is Ephesians 2:10. It speaks of how God has a plan for our lives—that our souls come pre-equipped with a longing to create and to do good works.

> For we are what he has made us, created in Christ Jesus for good works, which God prepared beforehand to be our way of life. (Ephesians 2:10)

God has made us. God has created us. And we are created for *good* works. All of this God had in mind even before your parents, or those who raised you, knew you.

Lectio divina is an ancient practice in which you take a passage of Scripture, usually not more than a few verses, and read them slowly three times, with long pauses between. The slow pace and the pauses allow the Spirit to "highlight" a word or phrase that stands out to you. Take these two powerful passages, Psalm 139:13-16 and Ephesians 2:10, and read them slowly, with an inner awareness of any words or phrases that stand out to you. This is often a "word" from the Holy Spirit that God has in mind specifically for you.

Lectio divina is one of my favorite approaches to the Bible. It is a great exercise to experience that God is intimately interested in our lives, and is intricately connected to us in the present moment. When you combine the practice of God speaking in the present moment regarding things from our past, it can be very powerful.

Once a word or phrase becomes highlighted in some way (an inner consonance, perhaps), write the word or words down in a journal or notepad. The highlighted word or words can change during the second and third readings. If that is the case, write down those words as well. Once you are through, pause for a moment of silence. Then look at the words or phrases and ask God what they might mean for you now, in this moment. Perhaps God will want to speak to you a word about your own unique situation. But either way, I am certain that God wants to speak this word to you: you are wanted, more wanted than you know, by the God who made you and has never allowed you out of his sight.

four

YOU ARE LOVED

Two questions haunt every human life," writes Andy Crouch. "The first: *What are we meant to be?* The second: *Why are we so far from what we're meant to be?*" I spent most of my life—including my life as a Christian, an ordained minister, and an author of books on the Christian life—haunted by that gap between who I believed I was meant to be and who I actually was. The haunting gap I lived with made it almost impossible to believe I was loved.

Years of practicing the spiritual disciplines, hours of study, and reading countless books on the Christian life had failed to convince me that I was loved by God. I sensed there was a problem in my soul that I could not solve. This is what led me to seek counseling; my soul needed some restoration. I was filled with a lot of shame that I could not *will* my way out of. I am grateful I reached out for help. It was one of the most difficult things I have ever done and one of the best things I have ever experienced.

In one of my first sessions my therapist, Michael, asked if I knew the source of my shame. I told him about an experience that was painful and puzzling to me. It involved my father, who I know loved me very much but was not great at communicating it. I told Michael a story about when I was in high school. I was an outstanding basketball player, and one particular weekend I had scored fifty-one points in two games, twenty-five on Friday night, and twenty-six on Saturday night. I came home excited for how well I had played.

When I walked into the living room, my dad was sitting on the couch deep in thought. I was not greeted with a high-five or a hug or a "Great game!"

Instead my dad said, "Did you know you missed four free throws tonight?"

I said I was aware of it.

He said, "Do you know why?"

I said, "No."

He said, "Your feet were wrong. Your stance was off because of it. That is why you missed them."

I stood in silence, stunned.

"How did that make you feel?" Michael asked.

"I felt incredibly hurt. I mean, what more could I have done to get his love, his approval, to make him proud of me? It turned out I led the league in scoring that weekend. And yet, all I got was a remark about how my feet were wrong."

We know who we are only in relationship. We only know there is an "I" because there is a "Thou," another person who can tell us who we are to understand our identity. And we have a deep longing to be loved. Our parents are the first people we look to in order to hear those crucial words, "I love you . . . no matter what you do." Many parents fail to offer those words in ways we need to hear them, to love us in the way we need to be loved. And we falsely transfer this picture of conditional human love onto God. As the old joke says, "God made man in His image, then man returned the favor."

We assume God is just like us. Just a really big parent who only loves us when we are good, whose love must be earned, and whose approval can easily be lost through sin and failure. For many years I struggled to believe that God really loved me and, in fact, that anyone could really love me. In my most honest moments, I could admit to myself that I struggled with self-hatred.

FALSE NARRATIVE: GOD LOVES YOU CONDITIONALLY

Just as we are made with a longing to be wanted and desired, we also deeply want to be loved without condition. We can never fully find wellness in our souls until we come to accept our acceptance in God, until we feel the embrace of the love of God. But it is difficult to feel that love. Unconditional love and unmerited acceptance are rare in human life. Because we are all human beings, flawed and finite, our loves, even the best ones, are flawed and finite.

Because we are loved conditionally by other humans, loved for what we do and how we look and what we have, we project this same conditional love onto God. And God knows more and sees more than any parent or coach or teacher, so we assume the scrutiny of God would make it impossible for God to love us. God is holy, God is pure—and we are not. Far from being loved without condition, many Christians believe God is disgusted by them, that they are "sinners in the hands of an angry God."

And yet, the entire Christian narrative rests on John 3:16-17:

For God so loved the world that he gave his only Son, so that everyone who believes in him may not perish but may have eternal life.

Indeed, God did not send the Son into the world to condemn the world, but in order that the world might be saved through him.

That passage clearly states that God *loves* the world, that God did not send Jesus to condemn the world. How did "angry God" narratives become so prevalent? And how can we ever come to believe we are loved in the way our souls long to be loved?

For most of my life as a Christian, it felt as if God was on a swivel chair. When I would repent, read the Bible, pray, go to church, I felt as if God was looking at me with approval. But when I sinned, when I failed to practice the spiritual disciplines, I sensed that God did not want to look at me, as if God were spinning on his chair until his back was to me so he did not have to look at me. So I would redouble my efforts and do something holy so God could make his face to shine upon me once again. But then I would sin again, and God would spin away again. My sin-confession-forgiveness-repentance-do-good cycle would repeat over and over, making God dizzy and me depressed.

Once I realized that God's love was not dependent on me or my behavior, the absurdity of this swiveling became obvious. I was able to see that this approach was a form of legalism, and legalism is superstition. I don't determine God's love for me based on what I do any more than seeing a black cat brings me bad luck. But we like superstition because it gives us a measure of control. If I can *make* God love me by reading the Bible more, then I can feel in control. This illusory control, it seems, is preferable to not being in control, so we hold on to it for as long as we can.

REASONS WE DON'T ACCEPT GOD'S UNCONDITIONAL LOVE

There are three main reasons it is difficult to accept the love of God: unaccepting parents, graceless religion in our churches, and exterior-based acceptance in secular culture.

> What are some of the reasons you have a hard time accepting God's unconditional love?

All of us wrestle with unaccepting parents, to some degree or another. As a parent, I know how difficult it is to communicate to my children that I love them, while at the same time working diligently to make them better. We hear the word *no* far more than *yes* in our childhood. Good parents are all trying to teach good manners, right behaviors, and encourage success in their kids. The common method is to punish bad behavior ("go to your room," "no dessert for you") to make it stop, and to reward good behavior ("you got an A; let's get ice cream") to encourage more success. We hear this so much it becomes deeply ingrained, and we come to believe that love is based on our performance.

Second, it is difficult to accept God's love for us as "graceless religion" creates "graceless Christians." There is a general sense that God is disappointed with us at best, and downright angry at us at worst. Philip Yancey was asked this question by former president Bill Clinton, "Why do Christians hate so much?" This inspired Yancey to write his wonderful book, *What's So Amazing About Grace?* It is ironic that a religion whose foundation is stated as "God so loved the world" could become a religion of so much judgment. When God is portrayed from pulpits to Sunday school rooms as a God who "punishes bad little girls and boys," it is hard to imagine a God who knows our every sin and loves us still.

A third reason why we fail to receive God's acceptance of us is that we live in a culture that appraises our value and determines our worth on the basis of what I call *the big three*:

- How we look
- What we do
- What we have

Sadly, we internalize this worldview ourselves. From the playground to the boardroom, from cliques to mean girls, from "likes" to "swipes," we are judged on our appearance, performance, and material wealth. And the problem is, there is always someone better looking, more talented, with more money and nicer possessions.

All three of these add up to a mindset that says, "I am not enough. I do not deserve love." As I felt that day in the living room with my father, we wonder, *Can I ever do enough to earn love? What do I have to do to find approval? What do I need to do to be accepted?* God can easily become the ultimate disapproving parent, the quintessential angry judge. Our only hope is to do better and try harder to get the not-loving God to love us. And yet, Jesus seems to be telling us a better narrative. In fact, as Brian Zahnd says so well, "Jesus didn't die on the cross to change God's mind about us; Jesus died on the cross to change our minds about God!"

And there's one more reason: I have found that I am my own worst critic. I live "under the tyranny of the ideal self," as Adrian van Kaam puts it. I don't want to be *kind of* kind; I don't want to be *sort of* smart; I don't want to settle for being *generally* good. I want to be, as we like to say, "the best version of myself," and for me that is nothing less than perfect, nothing short of the ideal me. As a result, I end up judging myself against a perfect me. The perfect me would never have an unclean thought or say an unkind word; the perfect me would never come in second or get a B, or even an A-.

I am not alone. Many of my friends also suffer under the tyranny of the ideal self. They live each day with a standard of perfection that is impossible to

> Do you find you end up being your worst critic?

meet and never allows them to rest. One of my good friends is bright and beautiful and talented, to the point that most who meet her are intimidated by her. And yet she feels she is "worthless," as she puts it. I asked her how this was possible, and she said, "Every time I did something that was not perfect, I had a father who let me know it and scolded me for it. Whenever I do anything less than perfect, I beat myself up pretty badly." When she spoke these words to me I felt a deep pain, not just for her but for all of us who suffer from this.

I vividly remember the day I discovered that the tyrant of the ideal self had been ruling my life. I had to see it clearly before I could begin releasing its control over my self-narrative. I could only do so by the power of the unconditional love of God—the truly *good news*. If God loves me as I am, who am I not to love me as I am? I began to laugh at my silly attempts to be perfect. It was freeing to accept the reality that I am perfectly imperfect. Perfection is an illusion, and it prevents us from accepting God's love for who we are, as we are.

TRUE NARRATIVE: YOU ARE LOVED BY GOD BECAUSE YOU ARE LOVED BY GOD

One of the reasons I love reading the works of the great Christ-followers throughout the ages is that amid vast historical and cultural differences I find points of connection. Teresa of Ávila's life and writings have inspired me since I first read her works in college. I love her candor and her passion. Teresa was a Spanish woman in the sixteenth century who entered the convent life as a Carmelite nun. She was a mystic who experienced deep connections with God in contemplative prayer. But she also wrestled with doubt and shame. Daniel Ladinsky offers a beautiful interpretive rendering of one of Teresa's poems about her experience of God's love titled, "He Desired Me So I Came Close."

> When I first heard his courting song, I too
> > looked at all I had done in my life
> > > and said,
> "How can I gaze into His omnipresent eyes?"
> > I spoke those words with all
> > > my heart,
> but then He sang again, a song even sweeter,
> and when I tried to shame myself once more from His presence,
> God showed me his compassion and spoke a divine truth,
> > "I made you, dear, and *all I make is perfect.*
> > Please come close, for I
> > > desire
> > > you."

Teresa's poem captures the hesitancy we have in accepting the love of God. She looked at what she had done and wondered how she could look into God's omnipresent eyes, eyes that have seen everything we have ever done—including our worst sins.

But what does God do? God sings! God sings to her "a song even sweeter." But what does Teresa do? She tries to shame herself once more. But God gets the last word: "I made you, dear, and all I make is perfect." God does not say, "All I make *can be* perfect." God says, "All I make *is* perfect." But this perfection is not the morally impeccable, flawless performance kind of perfection I used to pursue. This has to do with the perfection of our *being*, not our *doing*. As made by God, we are made exactly as God intended, and in this sense we can say we are "perfect."

> We can be perfect in our being, even when not perfect in our doing, because we are made exactly as God intended.

I love how the poem ends: "Please come close, for I desire you." This is perhaps the most difficult thing for us to believe, those of us who lived for years with an angry God on a swivel chair. We can maybe accept that God loves us because, well, God is God and can do anything. But surely God does not like us! The God who spoke to Teresa is the same God who speaks to you and to me. Maybe we cannot hear it audibly, but if we are honest, we can hear it in the cry of our hearts, the longing that we desperately have for this to be true.

One of the most powerful statements in the Bible is this: "God is love" (1 John 4:8). Three little words: God is love. Notice that it does not say, "God loves"—it says, "God *is* love." This means that love is not something God does at one time and does not do at another. Peter van Breeman explains, "If we think of God as a person who can divide his love, then we are thinking not of God but of ourselves. God is perfectly one, the perfect unity. We *have* love, but God *is* love. His love is not an activity, it is his whole self," because God is triune, three persons who are in an eternal relationship of love.

This is foreign to us because human love is divided. We can and do divide our love. We love sometimes, and sometimes we do not love. But that is not possible for God. The Greek words for this verse are *theos agapē estin*, literally "God love is." What kind of love is the love of God? It is *agape* love. There are four common Greek words for love, all describing different kinds of love (*eros*, romantic or sexual love; *phileō*, friendship love; *storgē*, family love). Agape is "love that wills the good of another," to use Dallas Willard's definition. God's love is agape love because God always wants the best for us and will go to any length, even self-sacrifice, for our well-being.

But God's love for us is also *phileō* (Jesus said in John 15:15 [CEB], "I call you friends") and we are members of God's family (*storgē*), and God's love for us is also erotic, though not sexual, as seen in the last three words of Teresa's poem: "I desire you." Saint Bernard of Clairvaux wrote dozens of sermons on the Song of Solomon, comparing the love between lovers in that book of the Bible to the love between us and God. My point is that God loves us in every possible way love can be expressed. The best love felt between friends, the most passionate love between lovers, the most committed love between family members, are all reflections of God's love. What is different about God's love is that it is complete and never-ending. Passionate love wanes, family love can be strained, and friendship love does not always endure. The love of God is unlimited and eternal. It is the love we have all been longing for.

> **Reflect on the fact that you can do nothing to change God's love for you.**

A few years ago I dug up an old tape of one of Henri Nouwen's talks, one that had spoken deeply to my heart so many years ago and sustained me in ways I never knew. I listened to the talk anew and found my heart soaring once again. Henri preached,

> We love because he *first* loved us. You and I are called constantly to claim that first love. The spiritual life is a life in which you more and more hear that Voice that says, "I have called you from

all eternity. I have loved you from all eternity. You belong to Me. And I am your lover. And I love you not because you do good things. Not because you have a lot of things. Not because people speak well about you, not because you are so exciting or have so many talents. *I love you because I love you because I love you.*"

The Spirit spoke anew to me through this old talk, as if Henri was speaking to me from the other side of the veil.

BELIEVING YOU ARE LOVED

And yet it is hard to believe we are the beloved. Love like this is so immense that it is difficult to bear, as William Blake wrote: "And we are put on earth a little space, / That we may learn to bear the beams of love." We must learn to "bear" love because it is hard to accept being really loved in this way. I find the love of God to be overwhelming. In many ways, my need to hear that I am loved by God is greater than I can understand, and yet God's love is also greater than I can accept. This is where the vicarious humanity of Jesus is so crucial. Jesus became human in order to do for us what we could not do for ourselves. As the early church father Irenaeus (AD 130-202) said so clearly: "Because of His measureless love He became what we are in order to enable us to become what He is."

Jesus does for us what we could not do on our own, and that includes *believing we are God's beloved daughters and sons.* Jesus, in his full humanity, has done this vicariously for us. We struggle to believe that we are the beloved because of many voices that shout that we are "no good," or "not enough." Jesus faced this struggle, and he succeeded in believing he was the beloved on our behalf. According to theologian Thomas Smail, "Jesus needed, not once, but again and again at each stage of his mission and each crisis in his living and dying, a freshly confirmed knowledge of his own identity."

At Jesus' baptism, which marked the beginning of his ministry, Jesus heard these words: "This is my Son, the Beloved, with whom I am well pleased" (Matthew 3:17; Mark 1:11; Luke 3:22). My friend

Trevor Hudson points out, "In stark contrast to ourselves, when Jesus needed to know who he was, he listened to his Father's voice, trusted that voice and claimed its truth for his own life." If Jesus needed to hear, again and again, that he was God's beloved in whom God was well pleased, then there is nothing wrong or weak about us needing to hear it as well.

Jesus listened to the voice of the Father *for us*. You and I will fail to do this perfectly. We may believe it one day, then deny it the next. Jesus has listened and believed on our behalf. Jesus even faced the temptation to define himself on the valuation system of this world: what we do, what we have, what others say of us. The same Spirit who descended on Jesus at his baptism led Jesus into the wilderness to be tempted (Mark 1:12). Right after hearing, "You are my beloved Son, in whom I am well pleased" Jesus went into the desert to face Satan's temptations to prove he was worthy of being loved. "'Turn stones into bread . . . jump from a high tower . . . bow to me and you'll be rich and powerful,' the Enemy whispered. Jesus was clear in his response: 'I don't have to prove that I am worthy of love. I am the Beloved of God, the One on whom God's favor rests.'" When I fail to believe I am the beloved—and I often do—I am comforted in knowing that Jesus always believes I am the beloved.

The apostles knew this truth about our identity, and proclaimed it in their letters. Peter, John, and Paul, who wrote most of the New Testament, communicated the truth that we are the beloved in their letters, or Epistles. In eleven of those letters, the term *beloved* is used forty-seven times. Paul calls the recipients of his letters "beloved" eighteen times, John uses it ten times, Peter six times, James seven times, and Jude four times (in one short epistle). Here are two that I find encouragement in:

> As God's chosen ones, holy and *beloved*, clothe yourselves with compassion, kindness, humility, meekness, and patience. (Colossians 3:12, italics added)

To those who are called, who are *beloved* in God the Father and kept safe for Jesus Christ. (Jude 1, italics added)

The apostles learned that they themselves were the beloved—despite their failures and sins and betrayals—and they told the early Christ-followers that they were also the beloved. What is important to note is this: flesh and blood did not reveal this to them, but only by Jesus through the Spirit did they come to this understanding. But the frequency of this term, *beloved*, should alert us to the fact that the New Testament is unequivocal about our identity. We are sinners, to be sure, because we sin. But that does not negate our identity as beloved.

AN OLD TRUTH BECOMES NEW

I suspect that many of you reading this are saying, "This is not news to me. I have heard that I am loved by God." If this is true for you, I am glad. But it may be that you, like me, need to hear it anew, and hear it in new ways.

Imagine a child is walking with her father. The father picks her up, hugs her and kisses her on the forehead, looks her in the eyes, and says, "I love you so much. You are so precious to me. I love just being with you. Do you know that?" The little girl blushes and smiles and kisses her dad on the cheek. So here is a question: Did she learn anything she had not known before? Was she given some new information about her father in that moment? Probably not. She is not given a new idea—but an old idea, one she has known and longs to hear, becomes new.

That is what the love of God is like for me. I need to hear it again and again. It is not new news; it is good news said in a new way. Every sunset, every act of kindness from a stranger, every piece of art or music that moves me, I now see as new ways God is loving me. Simone Weil said, "The beauty of the world is the tender smile of Christ to us through matter." I am learning to see and feel that smile every day—and I need to see it over and over.

One of my favorite verses is 1 John 4:19: "We love because he first loved us." God loved us first, by sending his Son for us (1 John 4:10). But, as Kierke-

Do you need to hear it said again in a new way that God loves you?

gaard pointed out, God does not just love us first *one* time. God loves us first every single moment of every single day. "When we wake up in the morning and turn our soul to You . . . when we withdraw from the distractions of the day and turn our soul toward You, You are the first and thus forever. And yet we always speak ungratefully as if you have loved us first only once." God is always present, loving us first each and every moment. I, for one, need to hear it again and again.

In the last few years, I have developed a deep love for 2 Corinthians 3:18. I believe it is the foundational verse for Christian spiritual formation. It is about looking into a mirror, but instead of seeing our face in the mirror, we see Jesus' face:

> And all of us, with unveiled faces, seeing the glory of the Lord as though reflected in a mirror, are being transformed into the same image from one degree of glory to another; for this comes from the Lord, the Spirit. (2 Corinthians 3:18)

In this spiritual mirror we see "the glory of the Lord." And "the glory of the Lord" is "the face of Jesus" (2 Corinthians 4:6). So what we see as we look into this mirror, by the Spirit, is not *our face* but the *face of Jesus*. And as we look into this mirror, beholding the glory of Jesus, we are transformed "into the same image." Love is the mechanism of change when we gaze on the face of Christ.

When we behold the face of Jesus, we see absolute love, and that love inspires love within us. This is how God communicates that we are his beloved. Hans Urs von Balthasar wrote, in what is one of my favorite quotes:

> In this face, the primal foundation of being *smiles* at us as a mother and a father. Insofar as we are his creatures, the seed of

love lies dormant in us as the image of God. But just as no child can be awakened to love without being loved, so too no human heart can come to an understanding of God without the free gift of his grace—in the image of his Son.

God, our Creator, the Creator of all, the "foundation of being," smiles at us. Read that again: God *smiles* at us. Can you imagine God smiling at you? This is hard for many of us who were raised with a lot of false, toxic narratives about God. And those toxic God narratives have led to a lot of toxic self-narratives.

But imagine God, in the face of Jesus, *smiling* at you. When by the power of the Spirit we are enabled to see it, the image of God in us is awakened, like a seed that lay dormant. Just as a child needs to look into the smiling eyes of a parent or caregiver to awaken love, so too we, in our spirits, need to look into the face of Jesus and see a smile. It is the face of Jesus, looking at us, that can transform us. That is because Jesus, unlike the others in our lives, *knows us completely* (sins and all) and *knows us accurately* (he is not prone to error), and is the only voice powerful enough to penetrate our hardened hearts.

> Can you imagine God smiling at you?

HE WAS LOOKING AT YOUR FEET

In the opening of this chapter I shared the story of how my father failed to acknowledge my outstanding performance on the basketball court, and instead focused on the little thing I did wrong. I shared this story with my counselor, who said, "I imagine you were hoping for something different."

"Yes," I said. "I was hoping he would say, 'Wow, what a great week, pal. You played so well! Fifty-one points!'"

"That must have really hurt," he said. I nodded yes. Then he said something that never occurred to me. "I think it is fascinating that he asked you about your feet."

"Why?" I asked.

"Because your father was in the stands looking at your feet. He was wanting so badly to help you, he was even watching your feet. He couldn't help you from the stands, but he was doing the one thing he could do—he was looking for ways to help you. That is why he asked you if you knew why you missed the free throws. He was trying to help you. But that is not what you heard. And he should have said what you needed and deserved to hear: 'What a great game—let's go have a steak!' and *then*, only then, should he have said, 'And hey pal, maybe later we can work on your free throws. I noticed something with your feet.'"

I began to sob as he finished that sentence. My dad really did love me, but he was not always great at showing me in the ways that I needed to hear it, and I was not always great at listening in ways I could hear it. This is one of the great things about our heavenly Father. We may fail to hear his love, for all the reasons I have written about in this chapter. But God keeps on coming to our games, and keeps on watching our feet, and never fails to love us in the ways we need to be loved.

Breath Prayer

And the LORD God formed man of the dust of the ground,
and breathed into his nostrils the breath of life;
and man became a living soul.
GENESIS 2:7 KJV

Breathe on me, Breath of God,
Fill me with life anew.
FROM THE HYMN BY EDWIN HATCH

The *breath prayer* flows to us as a practice of the ancient church. There is a strong and beautiful connection between our breath and the Spirit, portrayed in the sacred moment when God bent down to the earth and filled Adam's lungs with his breath, generating life into what was once dust. As we practice the breath prayer, we are attuning to the source of our soul's life, God's Spirit filling us with God's very own breath. We also savor our union with God as we notice that we breathe God's breath.

Just as there is a two-part movement to our breath, there is also a two-part movement to many breath prayers: an inhale and an exhale. Some of the prayers lend themselves to coordinating your inhaling and exhaling with parts of the prayer, but sometimes not. In all cases we simply attune to the natural rhythm of our breath as we pray the breath prayer, reminding us that our prayer life is to be as natural and as integral to our goings and comings as breathing. In this organic connection with our Source, intermingled with our daily lives, we can pray without ceasing as we breathe in and out all that is good and beautiful.

The best-known and most-prayed breath prayer is called the Jesus Prayer, originally prayed as "Lord Jesus Christ, Son of God, have mercy on me." Later, the words "a sinner" were added: "Lord Jesus Christ, Son of God, have mercy on me, a sinner." Sometimes the prayer is prayed in its simplest form: "Lord, have mercy." An added grace of praying the Jesus Prayer is that you are praying in concert with the universal church around the globe and with the cloud of witnesses throughout history.

Breath prayers that follow the same form as the Jesus Prayer begin with a name of God, followed by a supplication. For example, "Living Water, fill me." Or "Jehovah-Jireh, help me trust in your provision." Another option is for the second half of the prayer to communicate more as a statement rather than a request. So you could express your gratitude by praying, "Lord, my cup runs over." Other breath prayers don't follow this form but are wonderfully simple ways of praying, such as "When I am afraid, I will trust in you," or "You will never leave me nor forsake me."

Since this chapter is about the unconditional, unmerited love that God has for you, your breath prayer will open your heart to receive that love into your soul. The process of choosing a breath prayer is a practice in and of itself—it invites you to notice how your soul is, how you are longing for God, and maybe even how God is longing for you. As you choose your breath prayer, let awareness of yourself and of God be your guide.

You are invited to choose from the list of breath prayers below, or feel free to craft your own breath prayer. Please write your prayer on an index card or in your journal to remind you throughout the day or week what you selected. If you choose to write it on an index card, you can put it on your desk or on your dashboard, wherever you will see it frequently to remind you to integrate your prayer with your breath. Some people like to connect their prayer to an already established rhythm of their life to remind them to pray. For example, you could pray your breath prayer every time you stand up from your desk, or every time you get a drink or have a meal. Please find what works best for you.

Abba, I belong to you.
God is here, and God is love.
Shepherd, hold me.
Lord, fill me to overflowing with your love.
You belong to me, and I belong to you.
Jesus, help me receive your love.
Father, you love me because you love me.
Nothing shall separate me from the love of God.
Jesus, lover of my soul.
Help me bear your beams of love.

Feel free to choose a new breath prayer each day this week, or you may want to stick with one breath prayer all week.

The temple, as described in the Old Testament, was one of the places where heaven and earth overlapped and intersected, where God and humans met and mingled. We are now God's temples, indwelt by the Holy Spirit. Breath prayers are an invitation to experience the reality of your union with God through the Spirit who abides in you now in space and time. Breath prayers give you experiential access to the desires of God's heart for you.

five

YOU ARE MADE FOR GOD

When I was seventeen years old my life felt pretty perfect. I had two loving parents, great siblings, and a lot of friends. We were a solidly middle-class family, which meant that I never lacked for anything financially. And I was very athletic—I lettered in sports nine times—which also really helps in this world. I was an all-conference basketball player. I had experienced no real loss in my life at that time. In short, there was nothing that felt lacking in my life.

Until there was. I could not name it or understand it, but there was a feeling of emptiness inside of me. Something was missing, but I had no idea what it was. I shared my feelings with my basketball coach, who told me he had found meaning through the practice of positive thinking. He told me to get a book called *The Power of Positive Thinking*, so I did. It was in the self-help section of the bookstore at the mall. I also noticed a book on transcendental meditation and the blurb on the back said this practice was the way to inner peace and fulfillment. I bought both books.

I found the positive thinking book to be somewhat helpful, but my restlessness, my inner ennui and discontent, did not go away. I found

the transcendental meditation book more challenging and less helpful. It suggested I burn incense and sit in the lotus position and hum
a one-word mantra, which was strange and uncomfortable. I never
reached any bliss; I did fall asleep several times. I tried to hide the
smell of the incense, and I didn't talk to my parents about any of this
because they would have said to go to church and I found church
boring. I began asking some of my friends for counsel, and one of
them, Ned, said his uncle was a "spiritual man" he looked up to, and
he thought I should talk to him.

So Ned set up a meeting. We went to his uncle's house and I told
him about my failed search for a sense of true meaning and significance. He shared a little about his own faith. He was a devout Catholic who found meaning in service projects and going to Mass. Then
his eyes lit up as he told me about a new album he had bought—a
vinyl record—and asked if he could play it. I was a huge music fan
who owned the entire Beatles collection on vinyl, so I was excited. It
was Pachelbel's Canon in D, not what I expected, and I was no longer
excited—I didn't like classical music. When the music began playing, however, a feeling came over me, or into me; I am not sure which
to this day. It was more than peace or joy or hope, but it was some of
all three of them.

On the way home I stopped at the record store and bought the
exact same album. I went home and played it, over and over, hours
into the night. I pulled out a Bible my friend Tim had given me. I
started reading the Psalms for some reason. As I read Psalm 42, I felt
something stir in me:

> As a deer longs for flowing streams,
>   so my soul longs for you, O God.
> My soul thirsts for God,
>   for the living God.
> When shall I come and behold
>   the face of God? (vv. 1-2)

I sat and thought about God, a God I felt a longing for but did not know. I became quiet. I listened to the sound of silence, as I begged an unknown God to make himself known to me.

When someone asks me to tell my conversion story, this story is where I want to begin. Most people expect me to jump from my inner discontent to Jesus gently ambushing me six months later (which he did). But it was the evening at Ned's uncle's house, listening to a vinyl recording of Pachelbel's Canon, that my longing for transcendence found a glimpse of what it was looking for. Decades later, theologian Hans Urs von Balthasar gave language to my experience. According to von Balthasar, "The essential starting point for the human encounter with the divine is a moment of aesthetic perception, that glimpse of radiance, mystery, and meaning we see in a work of art or in the natural world." The God I longed for, as a deer longs for flowing streams, had blessed my soul in an unlikely way, through a vinyl disk and a needle, through vibration and notes and chords put together by a man named Johann who had died in 1706.

> Have you ever experienced a divine moment—a glimpse of radiance, mystery, or meaning—from art or the natural world?

THE LONGING FOR "MORE THAN"

What my embodied soul was longing for was the transcendent. The *transcendent* refers to that which goes beyond or rises above the things of the material realm, the physical world. What our souls long for is the spiritual. Most people know this about themselves. Quite often when I am traveling on an airplane and someone asks me what I do, when I tell them I teach in the area of spirituality, I almost always hear something like, "That's great. I am a spiritual person." I will also often hear, "But I am not very religious." Oprah Winfrey hosts a popular show and podcast called *Super Soul Sunday*, which is designed to help viewers "awaken to their best selves and discover a deeper connection to the world around them" by exploring themes and issues including happiness, personal fulfillment, spirituality, and conscious living.

Once in a while I meet someone who is happy to tell me that they do not believe in a spiritual realm. Only about 4 percent of the population consider themselves atheists, while 16 percent of the world's population describe themselves as having "no religious affiliation." If I get a chance to hear someone's story it often involves pain or hurt with religion or religious people. Still, the hunger for transcendence is a deeply embedded dimension of our embodied souls that will not go away. But many have been misled to believe that the deep longing for spiritual connection can be found solely in the things of this world.

FALSE NARRATIVE: PEOPLE AND THINGS
CAN FULFILL YOUR LONGING

The most common way the transcendent longing is expressed is the search for a soulmate—a deep, sexual, romantic connection with someone. There is a sense that we cannot be fulfilled without it. And many people are genuinely puzzled by the men and women who choose a life of celibacy.

The second most common way to fill the spiritual hunger is through money and material possessions. Money is a form of power—a ten-dollar bill is only a piece of paper with ink and is essentially worthless. But try ripping one in half in front of someone and watch them look at you in horror. This is because we falsely endow it with a power that is non-physical. The more money, the more non-physical power.

The third most common way we seek a spiritual connection is through the validation we receive from other people. When we receive affirmation, we feel a different kind of emotional jolt, a sense that we are known and accepted. A soulmate, material possessions, and validation from others address a *spiritual* need inside of us, albeit imperfectly. We may be—and likely are—completely unaware of the spiritual dimension of this longing.

We may even deny that these things fill a spiritual need or that we have a spiritual need at all. The denial can be maintained by repressing the spiritual side of the longing, but the longing itself will never go away. It will just seek another outlet. We will take some aspect of our lives and make it ultimate: our jobs, our achievements, our goals, and our bodies become ways to meet a spiritual need. The person who works eighty hours a week or the person who works out at the gym eight hours a day is actually on a spiritual quest.

Money, sex, and power have been the common substitutes for spirituality for thousands of years. Pornography, alcohol, and drugs are also shortcuts to the transcendent that, if we cannot have the real thing, will serve as a substitute. Alcohol is even called a "spirit," which is why Carl Jung once wrote, "Many people, lacking spirit, take to drink. They fill themselves with alcohol." People who are surfing for porn are, as my friend Michael J. Cusick has written, actually "surfing for God."

What we are really seeking is a connection with our Maker. This is because our Maker has created us with this longing—because our Maker longs to be connected with us. But the divine connection requires humility and trust, authenticity and vulnerability, and the pride within us rebels. If I make my career my god, I still maintain control. If I make my body an idol, I get to worship myself. If material success is my ultimate aim, then I get to possess my possessions: "Keep your hands off *my* things." The narrative that we can find what we are looking for through money, sex, power, and substances is an illusion, but one that is deeply woven into the fabric of this world.

Mass media, popular culture, literature, and even our educational system run on this narrative. Every product in every commercial is selling an answer to our spiritual longing, even if it is in the form of whiter teeth. Social media interaction is also a quest for spiritual connection. I once had a student tell me that he wished someone would create a virus that would "kill Facebook." I asked him why. He said, "When I go on Facebook, I end up feeling less worthy and more lonely."

Something deeper than seeing what our friends had for dinner is going on here. The educational system, of which I am a part, is also built on the narrative that "you should go to school so you can get a job so you can find a soulmate and buy nice things."

There is nothing wrong with education, or Facebook, or having a career, or going to the gym. And there is nothing wrong with wanting to find a soulmate. I have been very happily married to my soulmate for over thirty years, and I thank God for her. What I am trying to expose is a hidden narrative that within these aspects of human life we can find the answer to our transcendent longing. I am trying to show that the validation we crave cannot be found in how we look, what we have, and what we can do. Good looks, money, and talent are the currency by which we measure people's worth and life's meaning, but we are *spiritual* beings. And the culture we live in will tell us that we are loved if we have the right jeans, and rejected if we don't.

> Can you spot the hidden narrative in this world, that our longings can be fulfilled by the things of this world?

It is a competitive illusion. I don't just find fulfillment in having money; I want to have more money than other people. I don't just want a meaningful career; I want one that others esteem. I don't just want to be attractive; I want to be more attractive than others. Because the illusion is competitive, it also leads to bigotry and racism and classism. We do not see each other as spiritual, sacred beings, but as better or worse, richer or poorer, more or less educated. We have jobs, but we are not our jobs; we have possessions, but we are not our possessions—all these things are fleeting, temporary. In contrast, we are eternal, spiritual beings, embodied souls with a longing for something deeper than material things that rot and rust and can be stolen.

The false narrative is so deeply embedded that it takes a transcendence crisis to break us free from this illusion. A transcendence crisis occurs when unexpected events cause us to reflect on our lives. Perhaps a friend of ours dies, or our marriage falls apart, or we lose our job. These can be formative events. In my case, it was not a tragic event, but a sense of emptiness that created my transcendence crisis—even though I had no idea at the time what was happening. The common denominator of all transcendence crises is a deep longing for life to be meaningful, to have a sense of purpose, to feel as if we are a part of something profound, and it takes a crisis to wake us up.

TRUE NARRATIVE: ONLY GOD CAN SATISFY OUR LONGINGS

The longing for fulfillment is rarely debated; we all have that longing. The question is: Where will we find satisfaction? The deeply embedded false narrative, that we can find it through a soulmate, material possessions, or popularity and success, has a .000 batting average. No one has ever claimed they satisfied their transcendent longing through these means. In contrast, the longing for "more than" can be fulfilled in a relationship with God.

This is not to say that all religious people find the transcendent longing they are looking for. In fact, some religious practices actually prevent a deep, intimate

> When have your longings been fulfilled by God instead of by the things of this world?

connection with our Maker. The word *religion* comes from the Latin *religio,* which a means "to connect." At their best, religious practices are a means of connection to a higher power. But God is a consuming fire. Interaction with the Trinity will involve surrender and purification. As George MacDonald wrote, "Love loves unto purity." To connect with the Trinity is to go into a secret place and lock the door: "Go into your room and shut the door and pray to your Father who is in secret" (Matthew 6:6). But, as Jesus warned, some people simply want to be seen, to be thought of as pious, and their practices are more for show than for intimacy with God.

Still, the spirit within us, that part of our souls that is able to experience God, will persist in its search. It will never be satisfied with going through the motions. The void is too vast to be filled with anything other than God. And whereas God created this void in all of us, he did so in order to fill it completely and to satisfy our deepest longings with the perfect love of the Trinity. What we are searching for cannot be measured or fully quantified by our senses or by the sciences. But we all know it when we find it, even if only for a moment. Because the longing itself is a power, a dynamic, a *gifted disrupter* that will shake us out of our complacency and drive us deeper into the heart of God.

THE SPIRITUAL DIMENSION

This spiritual longing is a dimension of our souls—we are born with it. It is a preformed and undeniable dimension of our lives. It is what makes us distinctly human.

In all creation we alone are made in God's image, and relationship with God is the only thing that will meet this profound longing. This longing is the driving force of human life that propels us to reach higher and try harder. It is the enduring source of all great art, and the driving force of space exploration. The transcendent dimension is the motivating power behind every sonnet, and what makes us tingle at a beautiful sunset or elegant sonata. It is what brings us to our feet at the sight of a great feat: Michael Jordan scoring fifty points (I actually saw this once). Humans are longing for the "more than." Powerful hints of it can be found in a great film, or a piece of music, or a walk in the woods. We feel, for a moment, that there is something larger happening than just what we can see and touch.

The transcendent longing, the longing for the more than, is ultimately a longing for God. The hunger is so vast that it can only be met by something limitless. The transcendent yearning built into our souls is a desire for God. The Scriptures give voice to this longing:

> Your name and your renown
> > are the soul's desire.
> My soul yearns for you in the night,
> > my spirit within me earnestly seeks you. (Isaiah 26:8-9)

The soul's desire, the soul's yearning, is for the living God.

Saint Augustine, writing in the fourth century, described the transcendent dimension this way: "Thou hast made us for thyself, O Lord, and our heart is restless until it finds its rest in thee." God designed us with a deep longing that manifests itself in restlessness. And the restlessness will persist until we find that inner connection with God—the God who has been pursuing us through our longing.

The seventeenth-century mathematician, scientist, and philosopher Blaise Pascal also described the inner longing:

> This craving, . . . he tries in vain to fill with everything around him, though none can help, since this infinite abyss can be filled only by God himself.

The "infinite abyss" cannot be filled by any of the things we think will fill that void. It cannot be fulfilled by anything other than "God himself."

The transcendent dimension is a built-in, factory-included potency that is always present, even if it is not acknowledged. It is the deepest part within our embodied souls, and the least visible. It is directing our lives even if we are unaware. As Dallas Willard has written, "'Spiritual' is not just something we ought to be. It is something we are and cannot escape." It is influencing us even if we have

> What are some things that make you aware of the transcendent dimension?

not named it; it is unfolding within us every day; it sparks our greatest dreams, and fuels our greatest accomplishments. It is the source of the deep, inward intuitions that guide us.

Our spirits have a built-in *divine* receptivity. It is the infinite abyss Pascal described. It is the reason the Spirit can bear witness with our spirit: "You have received a spirit of adoption. When we cry, 'Abba! Father!' it is that very Spirit bearing witness with our spirit that we are children of God" (Romans 8:15-16). For me, the longing I felt, which could not be met by positive thinking or chanting a mantra, was finally met when I encountered Jesus on the pages of the Gospels. The Holy Spirit filled the Christ-form of my soul. My embodied soul found its rest in Jesus.

Jesus said, "God is spirit, and those who worship him must worship in spirit and truth" (John 4:24). God is spirit, and you and I have a spirit; it is how we connect to God. And it is how we connect to goodness, nobility, truth, and beauty. Humans cultivate those things because we are human, because we are unceasing spiritual beings. And Jesus was human and spiritual, as we are.

I studied how Jesus practiced the spiritual disciplines, searching the Gospels for clues about how he connected to God through reading the Scriptures (he clearly knew them), about worship (he went to the synagogue), and about his prayer life. What struck me the most was Jesus' private prayer practice and how frequently we are told that he prayed. In Luke's Gospel alone we are told that Jesus would "withdraw to deserted places and pray" (Luke 5:16). Luke records *twelve* instances of this. Why would Luke tell us this so many times? I think because it was a central part of his life—Jesus entered solitude in order to engage with the Father.

And Jesus was clearly aware of the false narrative that we can find the answer to our longing in the things of this world. He told a rich young ruler to give away his possessions, not because possessions are bad, but because the young man was possessed by his possessions and would never find what he was looking for in them. Jesus stood up to the devil in the desert, who tried to tempt him with power and earthly wealth and validation. He said no; he said no for us and on our behalf. And now we can do the same. We can say no to the treasures of earth so we can say yes to the treasures of heaven. God can and does bless us with various earthly treasures, but seeking them as ends in themselves will leave us empty and unfulfilled. In contrast, viewing them as means to the end of loving and glorifying God will bring us joy—seeking the treasures of heaven will satisfy our souls.

TRANSCENDENT MIND, WILL, MEMORY

How does the transcendent dimension work in our everyday lives? We have been given a mind that is capable of receiving the directives of the transcendent dimension. Paul encourages the Colossians to set their minds on things above (Colossians 3:2), and he encourages the Philippians to think about "whatever is true, whatever is honorable, whatever is just, whatever is pure, whatever is pleasing, whatever is commendable, [anything of] excellence and . . . worthy of praise" (Philippians 4:8).

Our minds are designed to take in the things of God. This is why Paul said to set our minds on the Spirit—our minds are built to receive transcendent directives. Think about a time you listened to a sermon and caught an insight, or read the Bible and a word or phrase came alive and started a chain reaction of new ideas about God and the kingdom of God. Our minds are the primary place God interacts with us. We have the ability to apprehend and appraise divine things. Jesus had this ability as well: "Let the same *mind* be in you that was in Christ Jesus," Paul writes (Philippians 2:5, italics added).

We also have a transcendent will. Our will is our capacity to choose, to decide, and to act. We are endowed with the ability to make things happen. So when we apprehend a divine directive, such as "trust in the Lord," we begin to trust God as seen in our actions, and this is done by our will. Our will *decides*, and by our will we *persevere.* We need the consent of our mind and our will to accomplish great things for God.

God has also endowed us with the ability to remember. Saint Augustine wrote extensively about the divine gift of memory. We use our memory all of the time. As I write, I am remembering the meaning of every word I type. I learned what "memory" means, and I remembered it. The transcendent dimension of our memory involves our ability to imagine. We have the ability to conceive of things because of our memories. When we planted a new church twenty-five years ago, my colleague Jeff Gannon and I imagined what this new church could be like on the basis of other churches we remembered.

We did not build the church out of nothing. In our memory we knew what churches are supposed to look like, and with our imagination we dreamed of what a new one might be. And we anticipated with great enthusiasm what this church might be. Now, looking back over twenty-five years of life together, we can see how we used our minds and will and memory and imagination to do something great for God. Lives have been changed over this span of time: people have heard the good news, lived in fellowship with one another, and partaken of the sacraments that bind us together thousands of times. God gave us not only a transcendent longing, but a transcendent mind, will, and memory to make it a reality.

AWAKENING THE TRANSCENDENT

The first awakening of our transcendent dimension comes in infancy. When we look into the smiling gaze of our mother, father, or caregiver, the transcendent dimension is awakened. We realize we are a person, an "I," and that there is another person, a "Thou," who has connected with us. A precious smile occurs when an infant sees the smile of another smiling back at them—into their eyes, which are the window to our soul—that affirming gaze awakens the transcendent.

When a family pauses for prayer before a meal, a child begins to recognize the sacred aspect of reality. Transcendent inspirations are awakened by our environment: the sight of our mother lighting a candle, or a minister presiding over a worship service, or someone speaking about their experiences of God are ways the transcendent is awakened. In my own family there were moments the transcendent was awakened in me. When we took family trips in our car, my mother and father would often sing, and one song that really stood out to me was "Go Down, Moses." My dad singing "Let my people go," with his deep baritone voice, sent a quiver in my body.

Transcendent formation will depend on the quality of the spiritual life a child is exposed to. My mother had a deep longing for God that was real and stayed with me even when I was far from God, when I wanted nothing to do with church. She witnessed wordlessly to a deeper life that would one day become central to me. She never forced her faith on me. There was a silent appeal, a call I could not escape. I am grateful my own children have grown up as believers, and I hold out hope with friends whose children have left the faith that they will return. As the often quoted verse tells us: "Train up a child in the way he should go: and when he is old, he will not depart from it" (Proverbs 22:6 KJV).

My friend John likes to say that every Christian needs a "mountaintop experience" at least once a year. By mountaintop he means those times of spiritual elation, or strengthening—those moments, often on retreat or at a Christian event, when God seems incredibly near. My friend Mimi speaks often of those "thin places," as the Celtic Christians called them, where it seems as if the veil between heaven and earth is razor thin. I think there is a lot of truth to this. We are made for transcendence, and summit experiences provide a great deal of strength.

For many years I have hosted the Apprentice Gathering, a three-day retreat featuring great speakers and workshops all dealing with Christian spiritual formation. Every year something powerful happens, something that we have no control over and cannot compel to happen. At some point, the room we are in begins to feel like it glows with the presence and power of God. A kind of glory enters into our midst and makes the place and the people within it feel holy. When transcendent, God-seeking people gather together to experience God's transcendence, God shows up in powerful ways.

I think this happens also because we plan and prepare for it. Not just those of us who organize it, but the people who come. They have spent time planning to meet God. They have chosen to *detach* themselves from their ordinary, busy, distracted lives for a time in order to focus on their transcendent dimension. And in that context, something powerful happens. More often than not, people come home having been deeply spoken to by God. I used to joke that "God must only speak in the woods," because God is so vocal on retreats in the woods. Of course, it is not the woods that make it happen; it is because the people who go to the woods have set aside a time to slow down, be quiet, and be present.

The challenge for us is what to do when we come back from a summit experience. We enter back into the same routines, the same overbooked, loud, busy lives we normally live, and suddenly it can seem as if God went deaf. Our capacity to connect has not changed; the light of our transcendent dimension has not dimmed—our focus has shifted. The web of everydayness has taken over. The challenge is to remain open to the transcendent in our ordinary lives.

> List some ways you can remain open to the transcendent in your ordinary life.

NURTURING THE TRANSCENDENT

We cannot always live on retreat. We cannot always stay at the summit. But we can discover the infinite in the finite; we can learn how "to see a world in a grain of sand and a heaven in a wildflower," as

William Blake wrote. The transcendent dimension of our embodied soul is looking for inspiration and aspiration all of the time, but most of the time we neglect it. We have to train ourselves to see it.

Fr. Adrian van Kaam was a young priest in the Netherlands during the Nazi occupation. He lived through the Dutch Famine, also known as the "Hunger Winter" of 1944–1945. He noticed that in extreme deprivation, people could still connect to the transcendent. He found that the people who during times of suffering could still see divine beauty, could still see the glory of the present moment, and could attend to the epiphanies all around them, fared much better than those who could not.

He built his entire understanding of the soul during this fertile period. He came up with a phrase I love, "awe-filled attentive abiding." For Fr. Van Kaam, this meant living with "appreciative abandonment." Think about a small child watching a butterfly for the first time. They are filled with excitement and awe; the butterfly creates a sense of wonder and joy.

But as we grow older, we lose the excitement, the awe, the wonder, and the joy in such moments. Instead of appreciative abandonment, we train ourselves to think depreciatively. We become blind to the glory and instead focus on the negative. We see what is wrong, not what is right, about people and circumstances. All the while, we are postponing joy.

Transcendent presence in daily life does not mean we ignore our problems. It does not mean simply thinking positively. Nor is it a trancelike state of existence. Instead, it means lifting every problem, every person, every situation into the light of our loving God's ultimate meaning. It is not trying to eliminate our problems, but to elevate them. We see daily life, from laundry to committee meetings to cooking dinner, with an awareness that God longs to connect with

> When is the last time you experienced attentive abiding and appreciative abandonment?

us through all of it. Nurturing the transcendent means keeping our eyes and ears open to the wonder of each moment.

One Sunday afternoon my family and friends and I were out on our deck, enjoying the sun, playing a board game, listening to music, and laughing. I paused for a moment and tried to soak it all in. The wonder of these marvelous human beings suddenly hit me. I did not look at them as anything other than epiphanies of grace. Our new puppy, Wesley, began playing with our older dog, Winston. They rolled around in the grass and it made me smile till my face hurt. Then, without warning, our neighbor's barbershop quartet started rehearsing in their backyard. The sound of the human voices and the harmony of the bass, the tenors, and the baritone elevated my embodied soul. When it ended, our whole neighborhood erupted in applause.

Van Kaam writes, "Many people reach only incidentally a transcendent view of life. . . . *Few persons seem to live a life that allows transcendence to blossom forth and to permeate their formation as such.*" I want transcendence to blossom in my life as much as possible. Each day we can seize the Spirit because God loves to take our hand in every moment—we can nurture and nourish the good and beautiful transcendent dimension of our lives, and linger in awe at these moments of life until they blossom forth.

I love the poem "For Longing" by John O'Donohue. It speaks of how God longs for each of us and how that longing brought us into being. And it speaks of how our longing for God is but a reflection of God's longing for us. May this benediction, and the truth behind it, quicken your soul with wonder:

May you come to accept your longing as divine
    urgency.

worship

The soul has a transcendent dimension, meaning it has a natural longing for the more than, for something greater than ourselves. This transcendent dimension is responsible for our passion for art, beauty, literature, and meaning. But the highest expression of the transcendent dimension is worship. In worship we give ourselves over to something greater than ourselves. Worship is an extravagant admiration for and a deep devotion to some object we esteem. By this definition people can and do worship many things, from soccer to nature to rock stars to money. And yet, all of these objects of worship leave the worshiper feeling empty or let down.

In short, we were made to worship. But the object of that worship matters. And the only object worthy of our worship is our Creator—namely, the Trinity: Father, Son, and Holy Spirit. When we worship God, the transcendent dimension of our soul is energized and comes alive, and because it is our Maker, Redeemer, and Sustainer that we worship, our souls are nourished. There are many ways to worship God, but the simplest and most direct is simply to set our minds on God. The great Puritan Thomas Watson wrote:

> The first fruit of love is the musing of the mind upon God. He who is in love, his thoughts are ever upon the object. He who loves God is ravished and transported with the contemplation of God. "When I awake, I am still with thee" (Psalm 139:18).

The thoughts are as travelers in the mind. David's thoughts kept heaven-road. "I am still with Thee." God is the treasure, and where the treasure is, there is the heart. By this we may test our love to God. What are our thoughts most upon? Can we say we are ravished with delight when we think on God? Have our thoughts got wings? Are they fled aloft? Do we contemplate Christ and glory?

I love that question: Have our thoughts got wings? Our mind, when it is set on the good and beautiful God that Jesus revealed, produces "thoughts with wings." And our embodied souls are transported.

One worship practice I find very helpful is to do what Watson suggests—namely, to practice God's presence. This involves simply being in solitude and silence, and turning our minds upon God who is with us. In the stillness I remind myself of powerful truths—thoughts from above (Colossians 3:1-2)—such as these:

- God is upholding me from day to day.
- God loves me far more than I can ever know or understand.
- God is out for my good.
- God is all-powerful.
- God is all-knowing.
- God is all-loving.
- God is a consuming fire (Hebrews 12:29).

Simple truths like these can produce thoughts with wings, and set my heart and mind on things above, where Christ is. This is what the transcendent dimension of our souls desires.

Many people, including myself, find music to be a great way to connect to God in worship. Today we have access to so much great music through streaming channels. I am grateful that nearly all of the great hymns and praise songs are at my fingertips. I do not sing well, but when I am alone and out of the earshot of others, I make a joyful noise and sing along with these songs or use my hymnbook.

At other times I simply listen and reflect on the power of the words. The other day I heard a new version of "Be Thou My Vision," and I listened intently until the words and the music moved me to praise and doxology.

This is not the only way to worship. There are many avenues to worship, according to Richard J. Foster. He defines worship as "an ordered way of acting and living that sets us before God so he can transform us." In other words, we must be intentional. I have found this to be true. We have to plan for worship. We have to set aside time, and we have to prepare our hearts for worship. I find this to be true for personal worship, but even more so for corporate worship, especially worship in church. Ironically, I am often hurried and distracted and inattentive to God when I am in church.

Again, Foster offers excellent advice for helping us prepare for Sunday worship in church, which he says begins the night before: "Prepare on Saturday night by going to bed early." He also suggests we "gather early before actual worship service" so that we can be still and become aware of the presence of God in the sanctuary. This helps us to "let go of the inner distractions" that hinder us from worshiping God. Every time I have followed Richard's counsel in these ways, I have found my worship experience much richer and more fulfilling.

It is a good and right thing to give God thanks and praise, as we say in the liturgy. But we do not worship because God needs our worship: God deserves to be worshiped, and our souls are designed to worship, and it is our great privilege to worship—this is why we worship. It leads to wellness in our souls.

This week set aside personal time to worship, and plan ahead for worship in your church, coming with a sense of holy expectancy that God will meet you there, and the meditations of your heart and mind will take wing.

SIX

YOU ARE FORGIVEN

I had been in ministry for six years, and I was ready to quit. I was struggling with something I could not name. One day while driving home from the church, I turned on an AM radio channel and a Christian call-in show was on the air.

A caller was asking the show's host: "I really want to believe that God forgives me, but I cannot accept it. How can you know that God forgives your sins?"

The host responded, "How long have you been struggling with these doubts about God's forgiveness?"

"Ever since I was a child. I did something very wrong when I was young. Every day I have begged God to forgive me, but I just can't believe God has," the man said.

The host asked, "How old are you?"

The man said, "Sixty-two."

"Do you mean to tell me that you have been begging God to forgive you for over fifty years?" the host asked, incredulous.

The man's voice began to crack. "Yes, yes I have," he said. "And I feel I have wasted my life."

When the man named his struggle, I immediately connected. Unlike the caller, it was not a single act for which I could not feel forgiven—I lived each day with a constant sense that I was racking up a huge "sin debt" I could not manage.

Have you experienced
living under the weight
of a "sin debt"?

When I was in college, an older Christian guy who mentored me told me to "keep short accounts with God," which meant every time I sinned I needed to confess right away, so as to "clear the account." He said the secret to Christian living was what he called "spiritual breathing." When he sinned, he breathed out his confession, "Forgive me, God, for that bad thought," and then he breathed in God's forgiveness, "Thank you, Lord, for hearing my confession and forgiving my sin."

This did not work for me. My "spiritual breathing" became "spiritual panting" and eventually "spiritual hyperventilating." It seemed the more I focused on *not* sinning, the more I sinned. Eventually I assumed I was a lost cause. I was caught in the snare of a sin-confession-forgiveness cycle and I could not break loose. Suddenly, listening to the radio program, I sensed what was causing my despair and making me want to leave the ministry. I could not wait to hear what this radio Bible teacher would say to this man, or to be honest, what he would say to me.

The host then told the caller a phrase that hit me so hard I had to pull the car over to think about it: "Until you rest in the finality of the cross, you will never experience the reality of the resurrection." A spark lit inside of me. *What is "the finality of the cross"?* I wondered.

The teacher asked the man, "Are you a Christian?"

"Yes," the caller said, "I believe Jesus is Lord, I confessed him as my Savior, and I have gone to church my whole life."

"Great," the teacher said. "Then here is the good news. You already *are* forgiven. Forgiveness is not something you earn; it is something God, in Christ, has already done for you. Jesus has already forgiven all of your sins—past, present, and future—on the cross. God forgave the sin you committed long ago, and he has already forgiven the sins you will commit tomorrow. That is what the *finality of the cross* means."

Wait. What? The caller then asked what I would have asked: "Is this biblical?"

"Yes," the teacher said, and then the radio went silent. I lost the signal. But my heart wanted to hear more.

When I got home I turned on the radio and tried to figure out who this Bible teacher was. The radio signal was faint, but with aluminum foil attached to an antenna, I found the station. His name was Bob George and his radio ministry was called *People to People.* I learned he had written a few books, and one of them, *Classic Christianity,* led to an entirely new understanding of the Christian life. After that day I began listening every single day, with my aluminum-foil-covered antenna.

Like the caller, first and foremost I wanted to know if this teaching about the finality of the cross—the teaching that Jesus died for all people's sins for all time—was supported by the New Testament. The teaching that Jesus died for all of our sins is clearly seen in the epistle to the Hebrews.

> Look up these verses from Hebrews and highlight the phrase "once for all" in your Bible, as a reminder of your ultimate redemption through Jesus.

In this letter the author compares Jesus to the great high priest, who had to offer sacrifices day after day in order to atone for the sins of the people. Jesus, in contrast, offered his sacrifice for sins *once for all*:

Hebrews 7:27—Unlike the other high priests, he has no need to offer sacrifices day after day . . . this he did *once for all* when he offered himself.

Hebrews 9:12—He entered *once for all* into the Holy Place, not with the blood of goats and calves, but with his own blood, thus obtaining eternal redemption.

Hebrews 9:26—He has appeared *once for all* at the end of the age to remove sin by the sacrifice of himself.

Hebrews 10:2—Otherwise, would they not have ceased being offered, since the worshipers, cleansed *once for all*, would no longer have any consciousness of sin?

Hebrews 10:10—And it is by God's will that we have been sanctified through the offering of the body of Jesus Christ *once for all*.

Jesus does not have to offer another sacrifice, because of his one-time death on the cross (Hebrews 7:27). Jesus obtained eternal redemption for all, not with the blood of an animal, but with his own blood (Hebrews 9:12). Jesus *removed* sin by the sacrifice of himself (Hebrews 9:26). Jesus thoroughly—not partially or temporarily—cleansed us (Hebrews 10:2). And Jesus sanctified us through his body (Hebrews 10:10). And he did this one time, for all time. One time, for all people. One time, for all the sins, of all the people, for all time. How in the world did I not learn this in seminary?

After a few months of studying the finality of the cross and listening to the radio program, I understood that the finality of the cross is not the end of the process of salvation, but the beginning. Jesus forgave all of our sins so that "there is therefore now no condemnation for those who are in Christ Jesus" (Romans 8:1). He died for all of our sins so that the issue of sin would no longer separate us from God. We could now draw near to God, and grow in our relationship with God. The cross was not the end but the beginning of new life in Christ. That is why the radio host said over and over, "Until you rest in the finality of the cross, you will never experience the reality of the resurrection." The resurrection is the means of a new life in Christ, but it can be experienced only if the matter of our sin is settled.

I FOUGHT THE LAW AND THE LAW WON

What was it that was so compelling about this idea? In chapter five I discussed our innate longing to be connected to God. But for me, and I suspect many Christians, the nagging issue is, "How can I be made for relationship with God if I am a sinner?" After all, it is true that we have all "sinned and fallen short of God's glory" (Romans 3:23 CEV) and "the wages of sin is death" (Romans 6:23). How then can a person who sins ever dream of being in relationship with a holy God?

The good news that God had forgiven me—once and for all—was not only freeing, but also created the possibility that I could actually have a relationship with God. Not because of anything I had done, but because of what God, in Christ, has done for me. The good news is that Jesus provides us a way back to a fully transcendent relationship with God. Unfortunately this good news is sometimes hard for us to accept as *personally* true.

As I explained previously, I was haunted by the gap between who I was and who I wanted to be. I assumed God was constantly disappointed in me. I resonated with what James said in his epistle, "For whoever keeps the whole law but fails in one point has become accountable for all of it" (James 2:10). In my intense battle to keep the law, the law had always won. I lived with a great deal of self-accusation for not being perfect. In fact, someone once told me that I was "the most scrupulous person" he had ever met—and it was not a compliment!

I think this is why the finality of the cross was so freeing and life-giving to me. It was as if the pressure was off: Jesus had done for me what I could never do. This is exactly what Paul meant when he wrote, "But when the fullness of time had come, God sent his Son, born of a woman, born under the *law*, in order to redeem those who were under the *law*, so that we might receive adoption as children" (Galatians 4:4-5, italics added). Jesus had redeemed me from the law. Redemption is a price paid to set a slave free—I was no longer a slave to the law, which meant I was no longer a slave to shame and guilt.

The problem is not with the law. That is "holy and just and good" (Romans 7:12). The problem is with us. The law was given as a means to walk in God's ways, but the Israelites failed to keep the law, as we all do. They worshiped other gods, made graven images, committed adultery, coveted, and lied. The sacrificial system was the means of atoning for the sins of the people. If they sinned, an animal—a bull, a goat, a bird—could be sacrificed to provide forgiveness for the sin: "Under the law almost everything is purified with blood, and without the shedding of blood there is no forgiveness of sins" (Hebrews 9:22). Again, there is no forgiveness without the shedding of blood; sins were not forgiven by confession, but by blood. If you read through Leviticus 16 you can see how this worked.

Of course, there were not enough bulls, goats, and birds to atone for all the sins of all the people all of the time. So they were given the annual Day of Atonement. On that day the people would fast, and the priest would enter the holy of holies and sacrifice a perfect bull for the whole nation. Two goats would be sacrificed as well: one slain at the altar, the other sent away as the *scapegoat*. The priest took the scapegoat and placed his hands on its head, transferring all of the sins of the people onto the goat, who would then be paraded through the city and driven out into the wilderness, symbolically removing everyone's sins.

And then the people celebrated—their sins were all atoned for! But the bad news was that the next day they would sin again and those sins would add up, day after day, month after month, until the next year when the bull and the goats would take away their sins. This system was God's gift to the people to atone for their sins. But the word *atone* means to "cover up"; it does not mean to "take away." So when John the Baptist says of Jesus, "Here is the Lamb of God who *takes away* the sin of the world!" (John 1:29, italics added), he is signaling something new.

> What does it mean to you that Jesus "takes away" your sin, not just covers it up?

The sacrificial system was only a shadow of the good things God had planned. This is stated clearly in Hebrews:

> Since the law has only a shadow of the good things to come and not the true form of these realities, it can never, by the same sacrifices that are continually offered year after year, make perfect those who approach. (10:1)

The law and the sacrificial system were not the true form or the deeper reality, only the shadows. This system could never make perfect those who desired to approach God. The blood of the bulls and goats was only a shadow of the reality of the blood of the Lamb.

The same is true of the law itself. The law was always outside of us, always judging, never helping. The law, also, was only a shadow. God's true desire was to write the law on our hearts, so that it would not be outside of us judging us, but inside of us truly encouraging us. And it was prophesied by Jeremiah:

> But this is the covenant that I will make with the house of Israel after those days, says the LORD: I will put my law within them, and I will write it on their hearts; and I will be their God, and they shall be my people. (31:33)

This prophecy became a reality in the cross and in the resurrection of Jesus. The author of Hebrews repeats this prophecy from Jeremiah, saying that this new covenant is now established by Jesus— no longer will the law be our judge (Hebrews 10). It will now be written in our hearts as God's act of love, because the law, rightly understood, is "sweeter . . . than honey" (Psalm 19:10).

This actually upholds the law in its original intention. Paul, no doubt, heard people object by asking, "What then of the law?" when he taught that the cross was final. He writes, "Do we then overthrow the law by this faith? By no means! On the contrary, we uphold the law" (Romans 3:31). Imagine it this way: Let's say you try to instill right and wrong into a child. To make sure they know right from wrong, you put a copy of the Ten Commandments into their coat pocket. When they are away from you, they are tempted to break the commandments that are written on the paper—they want to keep the commandments, but they fail. Now imagine those same commandments are written "on their heart," meaning they truly embrace them. Now, when they are faced with temptation, they say no because it is the deep desire of their heart.

Salvation is not only the forgiveness of sins; salvation involves a change of heart. When we experience the abundant life of Jesus, sin becomes "slop," to use Dallas Willard's fitting term—it becomes garbage. When we have been set free from the guilt of sin, we are also set free from the power of sin. Salvation is about being caught up in a new way of living, of life with Jesus in his unshakable kingdom, being rescued from the kingdom of darkness and transferred into the kingdom of God's beloved Son (Colossians 1:13).

Jesus, then, is "the end of the law so that there may be righteousness for everyone who believes" (Romans 10:4). Jesus is the end in the sense that the law is no longer our judge, and Jesus is the end in the sense that the law has been completed by the work of Jesus on the cross. The very last words of Jesus on the cross are, "It is finished" (John 19:30). The Greek word for finished is *tetelestai*, which means "paid in full." It was the word people stamped on an unpaid bill once it had been paid. *Tetelestai* means the debt of our sin has been paid in full; nothing more needs to be paid. This is why the apostles said, "All the prophets testify about him that everyone who believes in him receives forgiveness of sins through his name" (Acts 10:43).

Jesus didn't cover up sin, like the bulls and goats did, *he took away sin*. In fact, thanks to Jesus the sacrificial system was no longer the means to forgiveness, and the bulls and goats rejoiced! But many Christians, including myself, have replaced bulls and goats with confession. I would never have thought about getting my "sin account" with God settled by sacrificing an animal, but I was fully comfortable with the idea of viewing my heartfelt confession as a replacement for the goats. But since "it is finished" I no longer need to confess in order to get forgiven, in the same way I do not need a high priest to put an animal on the altar for my sins.

FALSE NARRATIVE: YOU ARE FORGIVEN ONLY FOR THE SINS YOU CONFESS

The idea that we must confess our sins in order to be forgiven is a deeply entrenched narrative. So much so that when I have taught the finality of the cross (and I have done so for years), I have received incredible pushback. After a lot of study, I concluded that this narrative is based on one, and only one, verse in the New Testament. It is this: "If we confess our sins, he who is faithful and just will forgive us our sins and cleanse us from all unrighteousness" (1 John 1:9). There is not another verse in the New Testament that equates sins being forgiven on the basis of confession. This entrenched narrative is largely due to Christianity's roots in Judaism and the Old Testament, where, as we saw, there is no forgiveness of sins without the shedding of blood.

And yet, this single verse is responsible for Christians believing that the forgiveness of our sins is dependent on our confession. When I teach on the finality of the cross, invariably someone quotes 1 John 1:9. But here is the truth about this verse—it only makes sense in light of the verse that precedes it. First John 1:8 reads, "If we say that we have no sin, we deceive ourselves, and the truth is not in us." There were people in the early Christian community who taught that they no longer sinned, that they were enlightened and transformed and could say, "I have no sin." John is essentially responding with this: *The truth is not in these people. But if we confess our sins, meaning, if we acknowledge we are sinners, God is faithful to forgive us our sins.*

> Do you recognize the false narrative that God's forgiveness requires our confession? Or is this a new idea for you to ponder and identify?

And note how many of our sins: all of them. Simply saying, "I am a sinner," simply admitting that we have sin, enables God to "cleanse us from all unrighteousness." Not some unrighteousness, but all unrighteousness. When you read 1 John 1:9 in the proper context, it actually supports the finality of the cross. So what then of confession—is confession of no value? What is confession for?

Confession is of great value; it is for healing, not forgiveness. James 5:16 reads, "Therefore confess your sins to one another, and pray for one another, so that you may be healed." We confess in order to be healed—confession is the road to healing. In confession, whether to God or to a person, we bring our sins to the light and in doing so the power of sin is broken.

Ironically, after I understood and embraced the finality of the cross, I confessed more, and more often. But I have never asked God to forgive me again. That would be an insult to Jesus and his finished work. I confess my sins not to get God to forgive me, but to talk with God about why I sinned, what triggered me to sin when I knew better. I no longer ask God to forgive my sins—God has already done that sufficiently. I now ask God to help me *not* to sin.

TRUE NARRATIVE: GOD NO LONGER DEALS
WITH YOU ON THE BASIS OF YOUR SINS

After a year of study, I came to believe that this teaching about the finality of the cross was biblical. But did church tradition support this teaching? Did the great theologians and spiritual writers of the past hold to this view? I decided to ask the question to my mentor, Dallas Willard. First I wanted to see if Dallas himself believed in the finality of the cross, and second to see if he knew of other famous Christian leaders who believed it. I explained how I had listened to the AM radio preacher, gone to the retreat, and studied the Bible, and had come to the conclusion that Jesus died for all of our sins, once and for all.

"So, is this true? Is this biblically accurate?" I asked Dallas.

"Yes," he answered.

Then he uttered a line so moving I had to scribble it down on a napkin, and I have never forgotten it. "It is a wonderful thing to know that God is no longer dealing with us on the basis of our sins," Dallas said.

God is no longer dealing with us on the basis of our sins!

"So, you believe this?" I asked.

"Of course, and so did Luther and Calvin and Wesley," Dallas said.

I would come to see that he was right.

Martin Luther built his reforming theology on the idea of the Latin term *sola: sola fide* (only by faith), *sola gratia* (only by grace), and *solus Christus* (only by Christ). Salvation is all the work of God, and not of ourselves.

> Take a few minutes to write down "God is no longer dealing with us on the basis of our sins." Reflect and write down what this means to you.

John Calvin gave us the term *wondrous exchange*. When God became human in the person of Jesus, God took on our humanity. Jesus fully identified with our sinful state and felt the full assault of evil. Jesus is the bridge between us and God. In the words of theologian Thomas Torrance, Jesus took on every human form of suffering and alienation and "endured it with joy, *refusing to let go of God for our sakes, and refusing to let go of us for God's sake.* Jesus presented us also before God, so that we are already accepted of God in him once and for all."

And John Wesley had his heart strangely warmed by the finality of the cross on May 24, 1738. He went to Christian fellowship one evening, where he heard a man reading the preface to Luther's *Commentary on Romans*, and later wrote in his journal, "While he [Luther] was describing the change which God works in the heart through faith in Christ, I felt my heart strangely warmed. I felt I did trust in Christ, Christ alone for salvation; and an assurance was given me that *He had taken away my sins, even mine, and saved me from the law of sin and death.*" Most Methodists mark this event as the beginning of the Methodist movement, a movement that would turn England upside down in the eighteenth century and the United States in the nineteenth. Luther, Calvin, and Wesley came to believe, as Dallas said so well, that God was *no longer dealing with us on the basis of our sins,* a teaching so profound it sparked movements that have changed the world.

A LICENSE TO SIN OR FREEDOM TO LOVE

One time, after preaching a sermon on the finality of the cross, a man came up to me afterward and said, "You are a dangerous preacher." I really liked the sound of that: dangerous preacher. But seriously, I wanted to know what he meant.

He said, "If we are forgiven forever by the cross, we then have a license to sin."

I said, "Well, that is true. We can sin if we choose to. But let me ask this, how are you doing without your license to sin? Is that working for you?"

He paused, and then got quiet, and finally confessed, "No, it is not working very well. I am struggling with sin all of the time. I assumed that I needed guilt to help me not sin."

I said, "Guilt is not a good long-term motivator. The better motivator is love. I have come to believe that guilt only makes the problem worse. I feel so bad about my sin that I seem to want to sin more. But the finality of the cross has actually made me feel God's love in a deep way, and I am less inclined to sin."

He said it made sense, and I told him, "Your way isn't working. Why not give this a try for a while? Test it against what the Bible teaches, and then give it a try."

A year later he came to where I was preaching, but he had a new look on his face. He said he was living in the freedom of the finality of the cross, and his battles with sin were greatly diminished. The finality of the cross is not about giving us a license to sin all we want; it is about the freedom to let God love us and to love God in return.

If we fail to recognize that the issue of sin between us and God is over, it will be impossible to grow in our faith; it will stunt our spiritual growth. We will forever be working to "get right and stay right" with God. But if we truly believe in the finality of the cross, we can stop focusing on sin and start focusing on our life with God. I have come to believe that our spiritual formation is learning to give more and more areas of our life to Jesus by faith. Put simply, how can we trust Christ with our lives if we are unsure of his attitude toward us? When I embraced my complete forgiveness in Christ, a new energy came into my body and soul, and my desire for sin became less and less.

God forgave us all our trespasses, erasing the record that stood against us, nailing it to the cross (Colossians 2:13-14). Every

> Are you unsure of God's attitude toward you? What is your belief about how God views you?

time I hear the hymn "It Is Well with My Soul," my heart soars during the third verse: "My sin—oh, the bliss of this glorious thought! / My sin—not in part but the whole, / Is nailed to His cross and I bear it no more; / Praise the Lord, praise the Lord, oh my soul." Our sins, not in part but the whole—past, present, and future—have been nailed to the cross, and we bear them no more, forever.

In doing this for us, God made it possible for you and me to be made alive. This is what Bob George meant when he said, over and over, "Until you rest in the finality of the cross, you will never experience the reality of the resurrection." The reality of the resurrection, being made alive by Christ, can only happen when the issue of our sin is over. Now we can live as new creations and sing and dance in the kingdom of God's beloved Son.

Laying Down Your Burden

In the classic novel *Pilgrim's Progress*, John Bunyan writes an allegory of the Christian life. In it, he describes the journey of a man, aptly named "Christian," who is convinced of his sin and burdened by it. In an early scene, Christian carries a heavy load on his back—representing the weight of his many sins. He carries his burden to the cross, where he finds release and relief. Bunyan describes it this way:

> Now I saw in my dream, that the highway up which Christian was to go was fenced on either side with a wall; and that wall was called "Salvation." Up this way, therefore, did burdened Christian run; but not without great difficulty, because of the load on his back. He ran thus till he came at a place somewhat ascending; and upon that place stood a Cross, and a little below, in the bottom, a sepulcher.
>
> So I saw in my dream, that just as Christian came up to the cross, his burden loosed from off his shoulders, and fell from off his back, and began to tumble; and so continued to do till it came to the mouth of the sepulcher, where it fell in, and I saw it no more. . . .
>
> Then he stood still awhile to look and wonder; for it was very surprising to him, that the sight of the cross should thus ease him of his burden. He looked therefore, and looked again, even

till the springs that were in his head sent the waters down his
cheeks. . . . Then Christian gave three leaps for joy, and went
on singing:

"Thus far did I come laden with my sin,
Nor could aught ease the grief that I was in,
Till I came hither. What a place is this!
Must here be the beginning of my bliss!
Must here the burden fall from off my back!
Must here the strings that bound it to me crack!
Blest cross! blest sepulcher! blest rather be
The Man that there was put to shame for me!"

While *Pilgrim's Progress* may be seen by some as a simple story
written at the level of a child, the truth is that this book, written
when Bunyan was imprisoned for his faith, became a bestselling
book. In fact, by some estimates it is the second bestselling book of
all time after the Bible.

If this is so, why? I have been blessed by the book and taught the
book in college classes, and I have seen firsthand that it speaks truth
to the journey of many Christians. The burden of our sin is heavy.
And the release we find at the cross is one of the most freeing experiences we can ever have.

An exercise I have found instructive is to find something heavy,
like a bag of potatoes, a backpack, or a stack of books. Walk down
the hall and back (or even around the house) carrying it. As you walk:

• Think of the heavy item as your sins you are carrying.

• Ask, what specific sins do you still carry, even though God has
  removed them from you as far as the east is from the west?

• Name these sins you still carry, even if only from time to time.

• Let Jesus be a table, and unload your burden onto Jesus.

• Then walk slowly down the hall and back (or around the
  house) again.

- Notice how much easier it is to walk.
- Then come back to Jesus (the table) and thank Jesus for carrying your burdens, so that you no longer have to carry them, ever.
- Then take the walk again, imagining Jesus right beside you as you walk without the burden. Notice how this feels when the weight has been lifted.

Take a few moments to write about your experience and insights from this exercise.

seven

YOU HAVE BEEN MADE ALIVE

Not long after I learned about the finality of the cross, as explained in chapter six, I began teaching about it. But I also had learned that the once-for-all forgiveness of Christ on the cross was only one part of the gospel; the forgiveness of our sins was a cleansing that now made new life in Christ possible. I had discovered, through extensive study, that in Christ we have not only died to sin, but also risen to new life. With these powerful truths in my preaching quiver, I began speaking about the finality of the cross and the reality of the resurrection anywhere I could.

Because I was both professor and chaplain at the time, I spoke at chapel once a month. I preached one day with a great deal of energy and fire from the stage: "In Christ we are forgiven. Forever. Jesus died for all of your sins—past, present, and future. God, in Christ, has forgiven you. And God wants you to walk in that freedom." I felt a jolt of energy on that day, and it made me glad to be a preacher.

The next day there was a knock on my door. It was one of the students who had attended chapel. His name was Stan.

He said, "I heard you preach in chapel that God has forgiven all of our sins—do you really believe that?"

I said yes. Then I asked, "Are you a Christian?"

He said he was, in fact he had grown up in the church but never heard that particular message. He was intrigued but unsure if I was right. I told him I understood his concern.

"I hope you are right," he said.

I invited him to come to the Campus Fellowship meeting sometime, as I would be teaching on it more and unpacking more passages in the Bible to support it. He agreed, and he began to come every week.

Then a few weeks later he knocked on my door, but this time it was not a happy greeting. He came into my office and sat down without saying a word. He put his hands in his face and began to sob. I sat in silence and waited. His sobbing became intense.

Finally, he looked at me and said, "I am garbage. I am no good. I tried to kill myself last night, and I even failed at that."

I asked him why he tried to kill himself. He shared that for several years, earlier when he was just a young teenager, an uncle in his family, a man he loved and trusted, began molesting him. His uncle made him feel like it was his fault and that if he ever told anyone he would tell them that Stan had instigated it. So Stan lived in fear year after year as this man held power over him.

"I told him he could not do that to me anymore, and he threatened to go to my parents and tell lies about me. I decided I could not face that, and I could not face another day of him doing these things to me, so I tried to kill myself last night, but I couldn't go through with it," Stan said.

"I am so glad you didn't, Stan. We will find a way out of this, and you will find out that God has a lot in store for you," I promised.

We have excellent counseling resources at the university, so I helped him make an appointment and he began speaking about his abuse to a therapist who began a healing journey with Stan.

After a few weeks I noticed that he came back to the Campus Fellowship group. I was teaching on the reality of the resurrection. My text that night was 2 Corinthians 5, and I focused on this verse: "So if anyone is in Christ, there is a new creation: everything old has passed away; see, everything has become new!" (v. 17).

I used the illustration of a butterfly:

Just as the caterpillar has to "die" when it enters into the chrysalis, the cocoon, so we also die with Jesus on the cross. Jesus' physical life fulfilled the law. Jesus' physical death upheld the law. Jesus' physical burial was proof of his death to the law (the dead are no longer under the law). And Jesus' physical resurrection is what frees us from the law. That is why in Romans 8:1, it reads, "There is therefore now no condemnation for those who are in Christ Jesus."

Then I went on: "But that is not the end. If anyone is in Christ, then you are a new creation. You are now a butterfly! The old has passed. You are forgiven forever, and made new forever." I asked, "Who here tonight is *in Christ*?" Nearly everyone put their hands in the air. "And who here tonight is *a butterfly*?" Nearly everyone put up their hands again.

I looked over at Stan, and his hand was held up high. The next day Stan stopped by my office. He had a huge smile on his face. He said, "Now the gospel makes sense. It is not about what we do for God. It is what God has done for us."

I said, "You have it, friend! You'll make a great preacher one day!"

Stan smiled and said, "Well, I don't know about that. But I know this: I am a butterfly."

FALSE NARRATIVE: ALL THAT MATTERS IS GETTING TO HEAVEN

In the late nineteenth century, during revivals of the Great Awakening in the United States, the gospel message was designed to get people to make a decision for Jesus. It was based on one aspect of the atonement—the saving act of Jesus on the cross. It went something like this: "You are a terrible sinner; God is angry at your sin. But Jesus took your punishment for you. If you confess him as the Son of God and accept him as your personal savior, you can go to heaven when you die." It was reduced to a gospel for *hell avoidance*. If you did not want to burn in eternal damnation (who does?) then you would simply make a decision for Jesus, and the preacher would consider this as a conversion.

This narrative is not entirely wrong. We are sinners in need of forgiveness; Jesus did die to take away the sins of the world, your sins and mine. Jesus is Lord, and we ought to confess him as such. If we confess him as Lord, we can be assured that we will reign with him in heaven after we die. This gospel is not wrong, it is just incomplete. It is a gospel of *sin management*, as Dallas Willard taught. It is a gospel for the afterlife, but not a gospel for life—for *zoē* life, or the abundant life that Jesus said he came to give us (John 10:10). It is not a gospel that naturally leads to inner transformation, to discipleship under Jesus, and to being formed in the image of Christ.

If you ask a group of people, "What is the significance of Christ's death on the cross?" most everyone will say, "He died for the forgiveness of sins." But if you ask people, "What is the significance of Christ's resurrection?" you will get, in my experience, silence. I know this to be true because I have done it with many groups of Christians. Once in a while someone will say, "The resurrection was proof of his deity," meaning that Jesus rising from the dead proved he was the Son of God. And that is true. But the meaning of the resurrection is much more than that.

A better question is, "How does the resurrection apply to our everyday lives?" This question gets to the heart of the matter.

> How does the resurrection apply to your everyday life? Write in your journal what comes to mind.

TRUE NARRATIVE: CHRIST LIVES IN YOU

Jesus rose from the dead to impart new life to those who believe in him. Jesus lived a life we cannot live, died a death we cannot die, and rose from the grave, defeating death—something we cannot do. The issue of our sin has been dealt with on the cross—and it was final. Jesus died for our sins, past, present, and future. There is no condemnation for those who are in Christ (Romans 8:1).

But we have another, equally insurmountable problem: Our problem is not only that we are sinners in need of forgiveness; we are also dead people in need of new life. Jesus died in order to reconcile us to God—we are forgiven forever. Jesus rose from the dead in order to give us *new life*. Who needs life? People who are dead.

The fall of humanity, which happened in the Garden of Eden, resulted in spiritual death. Adam and Eve had only one commandment to keep, and that commandment came with a clear consequence: "Of the tree of the knowledge of good and evil you shall not eat, for in the day that you eat of it you shall die" (Genesis 2:17). They did eat of the fruit, and they did die. But they did not physically die on the spot; the fruit was not poisonous. According to Genesis 5:4, Adam lived another eight hundred years. So in what sense did they die? They died *spiritually*. And all who came after them would be the same: physically alive, but spiritually dead.

Paul explains it this way: "For as all die in Adam, so all will be made alive in Christ" (1 Corinthians 15:22). In what sense are we dead? We are dead to the things of God; we are dead to God "through the trespasses and sins" (Ephesians 2:1); we are dead to the spiritual realm. When someone is sleeping very soundly we say, "They are dead to the world." They are not actually dead, but they are dead to the world around them. The television may be blaring, people may be talking, but none of that matters—they are oblivious to it, they are "dead" to it. In the same way, we are born into this world with a soul that has been designed for God, but we are not alive to God. That is because we are under the dominion of sin.

But Jesus broke that dominion. He disarmed the principalities and powers. He nailed our sins to the cross.

> And *when you were dead* in trespasses and the uncircumcision of your flesh, God made you alive together with him, when he forgave us all our trespasses, erasing the record that stood against us with its legal demands. He set this aside, nailing it to the cross. He disarmed the rulers and authorities and made a public example of them, triumphing over them in it. (Colossians 2:13-15, italics added)

We were dead, but God made us alive together with him. He forgave not some but *all* of our trespasses (the finality of the cross). The legal demands are not standing against us. By faith, we have died with Jesus. The powers that stood against us—the law we could not keep, the sin we could not stop, and the death we could not defeat—were all dealt with once and for all by Jesus.

JESUS GAVE HIS LIFE TO US

Jesus' death established our reconciliation; Jesus' resurrection imparts our new life in him. This is why Paul can say such powerful and profound and life-giving truths as these:

> I have been crucified with Christ; and it is no longer I who live, but it is Christ who lives in me. (Galatians 2:19-20)

> But God, who is rich in mercy, out of the great love with which he loved us even when we were dead through our trespasses, made us alive together with Christ—by grace you have been saved—and raised us up with him and seated us with him in the heavenly places in Christ Jesus. (Ephesians 2:4-6)

> So if anyone is in Christ, there is a new creation: everything old has passed away; see, everything has become new! (2 Corinthians 5:17)

This is the missing piece of the gospel, of the good news, that so many people never hear. It is why so many Christians are walking around as "forgiven dead people," as "dead people walking," still trying by their willpower to shape up and do better.

Jesus gave his life for us so that he could give his life to us . . . so that he can live his life through us. The Christian life is not hard to live—it is impossible! Only one person lived the Christian life: Jesus. And he rose from the dead so that he could live in and through us. This is how Paul can proclaim, "I can do all things through him who strengthens me" (Philippians 4:13) and "I am grateful to Christ Jesus our Lord, who has strengthened me" (1 Timothy 1:12).

> Give an example of trying to live by your own willpower to shape up and do better. Can you surrender whatever it is so Jesus can live his life through you instead, because he has already taken away your sins?

When we acknowledge Jesus as our Lord, and surrender our lives to Christ, we are awakened into a life with God: "Very truly, I tell you, no one can see the kingdom of God without being born from above" (John 3:3). We can now interact with the kingdom of God; it was a world we were dead to but now we are alive to the kingdom. When I first surrendered my life to Christ, a number of wonderful things happened. I would learn that I was not special or gifted or different from other Christians, but that the experience I had was normative, because these capacities are built into the *good and beautiful you.*

Here are some of the things that happen to us when we are made "alive together with Christ" (Ephesians 2:5):

> If you were to make a list of what happens when we are made "alive together with Christ," what would be included?

- Our spiritual senses awaken.
- The Bible begins to make sense.
- We hunger to be in fellowship.
- Former sinful actions begin to leave us empty.
- We feel a peace that passes understanding.

When I was journeying into faith late in high school, a good friend who was a Christian gave me a Bible. It was the old *Living Bible*, which was the easiest to understand of all Bibles. But still I found it puzzling. It was also not great that my friend suggested I begin with Acts and the Psalms. But after I became a Christian my parents bought me a King James Bible—in many ways the most challenging translation, as it was written over four hundred years ago. But amazingly, I was able to read and understand it.

My spiritual senses had been awakened, and the truths of the Bible began to make sense. Also to my surprise, I suddenly had a deep longing to be with other Christians. This was surprising because I detested church as a kid, and I found most Christians a bit odd. But after my conversion I wanted to be with these peculiar people (1 Peter 2:9 KJV). Because, I would learn, they were now my family of faith. I was not a huge partier, but after my conversion parties felt hollow. I was not immune to sin by any means, but sin felt different now. Finally I felt a peace I had never felt before. Even when my life was uncertain I felt peace—I did not know where my life was going, but wherever I was going I was going with God.

JESUS RESTORES THE IMAGE OF GOD IN US

I am fascinated by the work of those who restore art. There was a painting, completed in 1660, by Charles Le Brun. The 355-year-old family portrait was covered in badly tinted varnish and had a lot of scratches and structural damage that had nearly split the painting in half. It took ten months for the restorer, Michael Gallagher, to bring the painting back to its original form. He had to retouch, restructure, and revarnish in order to bring this painting back to life, back to its original form.

You and I were made in God's image. We are embodied souls, or ensouled bodies. Christianity teaches that our souls are never separated from our bodies. Our embodied souls contain the image of God. But what is the image of God in us? Some will say it is our ability to think or dream, our longing for beauty, or our ability to have dominion over things, as promised in Genesis 1:26: "Then God said, 'Let us make humankind in our image, according to our likeness; and let them have dominion.'" None of these are the image of God in us. Christ Jesus is the image of God: "He [Jesus] is the image of the invisible God, the firstborn of all creation" (Colossians 1:15).

You and I come premade to be conformed to the image of Christ: "For those whom he foreknew he also predestined to be conformed to the image of his Son" (Romans 8:29). The image of God is a part of our embodied souls, but it has been deactivated because of the fall. When we are raised to new life in Christ, the image of God is restored in us. We can now resemble the God in whose image we were made.

When we meet someone's parents, we can often see the resemblance. Sometimes it is uncanny. People say of our daughter, Hope, that she is a "mini-Meghan" because she physically resembles my wife. If all humans are made in the image of God, we ought to all resemble God. But if an alien were to come to earth and look at humans and ask, "What is your God like?" it would be absurd to say *God is just like the humans* who are made in God's image. Because apart from Christ, we are fallen and broken—cracked icons and distorted images.

The only answer to the question "What is God like?" is Jesus. Jesus told Philip, "If you have seen me, you have seen the Father" (John 14:9 CEV). This is how Jesus restores the image of God in us. By rising and giving us new, eternal life, the image of God is restored in us. A sincere Christ-follower, who is acting in love, compassion, self-sacrifice, and forgiveness, is the closest we humans ever come to resembling God. And even then it is not us, but Christ who is in us.

One of the great disappointments in our world today is un-Christ-like Christians. One of the leading causes of unbelief is Christians who are not living vibrant lives. I think the primary reason for the lack of maturity is a failure to understand the finality of the cross and the reality of the resurrection. In their place we have focused more on rule keeping and moral behavior, which are important but only as the byproduct of new life in Christ—not as a substitute.

Write down "The finality of the cross and the reality of the resurrection" in your journal. Reflect on these words and write what they mean to you.

In 2 Peter 1:4-9, the author lays out a challenge for Christ-followers to grow in faith, goodness, knowledge, self-control, endurance, godliness, mutual affection, and love. These are the marks of Christian maturity, as are the fruit of the Spirit (love, joy, peace, etc.). But these marks, these fruit, are dependent on our remembrance, our awareness, our confidence in the "cleansing of past sins" (2 Peter 1:9), and our trust that in Christ we are now "participants of the divine nature" (2 Peter 1:4).

> Thus he has given us . . . his precious and very great promises, so that . . . [we] may become *participants of the divine nature.* For this very reason, you must make every effort to support your faith with goodness, and goodness with knowledge, and knowledge with self-control, and self-control with endurance, and endurance with godliness, and godliness with mutual affection, and mutual affection with love. For if these things are yours and are increasing among you, they keep you from being ineffective and unfruitful in the knowledge of our Lord Jesus Christ. *For anyone who lacks these things is short-sighted and*

blind, and is forgetful of the cleansing of past sins. (2 Peter 1:4-9, italics added)

As long as we think we have *not* been cleansed and we are *not* partakers of the divine nature, we will be stuck trying to manage our sins and trying, by our willpower, to become like Christ.

When we come to understand our true identity in Christ, barriers to spiritual maturity fall down. Our formation in Christ cannot happen as long as we are disconnected to the life of Christ within us. Oswald Chambers wrote,

> The characteristic of the new birth is that I yield myself so completely to God that Christ is formed in me. This is not a command, but a fact based on the authority of God. The evidence of the new birth is that I yield myself so completely to God that "Christ is formed" in me. And once "Christ is formed" in me, His nature immediately begins to work through me.

It is the nature of Christ in me, the restored image of God in me, that is the secret to my maturity in Christ. And the world we live in is desperate for this.

OUR EMBODIED SOULS JUST WANT TO HAVE FUN

The *imago Dei* inside each of us, then, is the image of Christ. But what is that image like? What would it be like for you and for me to have Christ living in us? For years I assumed that this would be an eternal, cosmic bummer. I mistakenly assumed that if I gave my life fully to Christ, I would never have any more fun. In the words of Billy Joel, "I would rather laugh with the sinners than cry with the saints." I assumed all the sinners were the ones having fun, and the saints were sobbing in some sanctuary.

But Jesus said, "I came that they may have life, and have it abundantly" (John 10:10). He promised *abundant* life. He also prayed for his disciples, "I speak these things in the world so that they may have *my joy* made complete in themselves" (John 17:13, italics added).

Jesus came to give us his joy. Presumably, the disciples did not say, "No thanks, Jesus, we will pass. You are a dud. Your joy will not complete us!" They knew Jesus was a person of joy. How did that get lost in our day?

Dallas Willard wrote,

> The One who came to give abundance of life is commonly thought of as a cosmic stuffed shirt, whose excessive "spirituality" probably did not allow him normal bodily functions and certainly would not permit him to throw a Frisbee or tackle someone in a football game. But God is not opposed to natural life with all of its pleasures and pains and is even very favorably disposed to it.

What does it mean to have the abundant life Jesus brought? A central part of the abundant life is the ability to seize the beauty of this life, and to live with gladness as a result of it.

Do you agree that our souls cannot endure deadness? Why or why not?

Our souls cannot endure deadness; they were designed for an adventure, and sin is ultimately a dead end because it is inwardly focused. We have been falsely led into believing that spiritually mature people should not play, seek diversion, or engage in helpful amusement. But spiritually mature people are characterized by what they do, not by what they don't. God has designed us so that our joy would be full and complete, and that can only happen in Christ. A non-believer can have fun, but that is not the same as joy in abundant life in Christ.

The greatest adventure I have ever had is living with Jesus in his unshakable kingdom. Every day is an opportunity to watch God do some amazing work. Bishop Will Willimon once said, "The greatest sin Christians can commit is boredom." For years I found the Christian life boring, but that was before I learned about the kingdom of

God and an interactive life with God. We ask too little and attempt too little, because we think we are alone. But God is intimately involved with us and wants to empower us to live an abundant life of surprise. Your embodied soul was not made for sin, but for happiness and fun and excitement. And all those things can be godly. Holiness and hilarity are not opposed.

OUR SOULS ARE MADE FOR THE EASY YOKE

Jesus invites our souls into rest. He knows that life is hard. He even said, "In this world you will have trouble" (John 16:33 NIV). He did not say we *might* have trouble, but that we *will* have trouble. It is a mandatory fact of life. So he invites us into life with him in his easy yoke:

> Come to me, all you that are weary and are carrying heavy burdens, and I will give you rest. Take my yoke upon you, and learn from me, for I am gentle and humble in heart, and you will find *rest for your souls*. For my yoke is easy, and my burden is light. (Matthew 11:28-30, italics added)

Jesus invites us to take his yoke upon us. A *yoke* means two things. First, it refers to a rabbi's teaching; the yoke of a rabbi was his teaching. So when Jesus invites us to take up his yoke, he is inviting us to live into his teachings. That is why Jesus said to take up his yoke and "learn from me." We really can learn how to love our enemies and bless those who curse us and be free from anger, but not on our own.

The second aspect of the metaphor of the yoke is from farming. Animals are yoked together to harness energy. Two oxen pulling together are very powerful, as any farmer back then would have known. To take up the yoke of Jesus is to be united with *his* power. Paul knew this, which is why he said, "For Christ's sake, I delight in weaknesses. . . . For when I am weak, then I am strong" (2 Corinthians 12:10 NIV). Notice that he did not say, "When I am weak, *he* is strong"; he says, "When I am weak, I am strong." This is the secret of the easy yoke.

I spent two weeks in Australia working with ministers who had been learning how to live in the easy yoke of Jesus. Dallas Willard had been there many years earlier and taught these men and women how to do ministry by the power of Jesus, not their own power. At the end of my time with them, they presented me with a mug. It had Dallas's face on it, and a quote of his that read, "You Don't Have to Make It Happen." One of the ministers told me why they chose this saying: "Our work in ministry is very hard here in Australia. Dallas said this quote to us many times to remind us that we are not the ones who have to make it happen, but that we are in partnership with Jesus. He is the One who makes it happen." To this day I treasure that mug, and when I drink from it I smile.

Another of Dallas's quotes that he often said is this: "Do the next thing you know to be right, and expect God to bail you out." This is also what it means to live in the easy yoke. We simply trust the teachings of Jesus and put his words into practice (the next right thing) and then we trust God to bail us out if needed. For example, Jesus said we must not lie (Matthew 5:37). Life puts us in difficult situations where lying seems like a good option in order to avoid pain or gain pleasure. But if we tell the truth, for example, in a job interview as opposed to "spinning" the truth, we can then trust in God to help bail us out. If we don't get the job, we are not in trouble. We live in the unshakable kingdom. God will take care of us, just as he does the birds of the air.

Learning the secret of the easy yoke and learning that I do not have to make it happen has sustained me in ministry. I nearly killed myself early on in ministry, as many other pastors and church leaders do. If the devil cannot get you with the usual sins of the flesh (lust, money, power) he will get you through busyness, stress, and the pressure of thinking we have to make it happen. What I have learned is that Jesus did not come to help me serve God. Jesus did not call me into ministry to serve him; Jesus called me into ministry so that he could minister to others through me. Most of the time, this means I need to get out of the way.

YOU ARE A BUTTERFLY

Stan, the student who came to me many years ago to learn about the finality of the cross and the reality of the resurrection, was so taken by the image of being a butterfly that he told me it had become his primary way of thinking about his identity. He asked me if at our next Campus Fellowship meeting he could tell his story of abuse and how he had found strength in the midst of this suffering. I said sure. That next evening he gave his testimony, and there was not a dry eye in the room. Stan ended his talk by saying, loudly and proudly, "But I know who I am now. I am a butterfly."

A few months later, Stan shocked me by saying, "I want to talk with the uncle who molested me. I want to tell him that I have been forgiven and made new in Christ. And I want to tell him I forgive him."

I said, "That may not be a good idea."

"Why?" Stan asked. "God has forgiven me, and God said we need to forgive others."

"But are you ready yourself? And are you ready for how he might react?" I asked.

He said he was. I told him if he must do it, then I would prefer he do so with a trusted person.

As it turned out, the singer-songwriter Rich Mullins, who was attending the Campus Fellowship and had heard his story and was very moved, offered to go with Stan. His uncle denied any wrongdoing, but that did not matter to Stan. He offered him forgiveness—not just his forgiveness, but the forgiveness in Christ. Stan gave him his testimony and told him about his love for Jesus.

Stan graduated, and we lost touch for several years. Then one day I received a card in the mail from Stan. In it he said that he had become a Navy SEAL, and that he had gotten married and had a child, and he included his family picture. He thanked me for teaching him about the finality of the cross and the reality of the resurrection, and ended his note by signing, "Stan, the Butterfly."

if i were a child . . .

"Like the play of sunlight on water, joy shifts from moment to moment. Wild and free, scornful of rules, joy refuses to be pinned down and systematized in a book. Joy is not something to be written or read about, but lived." This exercise is an invitation to take a deeper step into the abundant life that Jesus gives through his life lived in us and through us.

Have you ever noticed how a person's home reflects their joy? If someone is full of life and joy, they tend to decorate their home in beautiful colors and with items that lift the spirit. Since we are temples of Jesus' Spirit (1 Corinthians 6:19) and Jesus Christ is not "a cosmic stuffed shirt," how might his presence living in us make us more alive? Paul even called Christ in you "the hope of glory" (Colossians 1:27).

Most of us lose the spark of life we had as a little child. As a way to let your embodied soul live more in sync with the abundant life of Christ in you, give yourself permission to experience the joyful life of a child. Jesus said, "Unless you change and become like children, you will never enter the kingdom of heaven" (Matthew 18:3). We will explore two aspects of the life of a child.

The first aspect is the reaction of abandoned joy a child shows because of something good and beautiful. If you ask a group of little kids who wants ice cream, what do you get? Squeals, laughter, exuberant energy! So you are invited to let Jesus' zeal for life well up within you.

If you have forgotten what that looks like or don't have good memories of that period in your own life, watch a little child blowing bubbles or playing with a puppy. You could do an image search on your phone or computer for "child playing in sprinkler." Notice the wonder and delight. Children wear joy all over their faces and all through their entire bodies. They don't just feel joy, they jump for joy.

The second aspect of a child we will connect with is curiosity. Children don't just wonder about things, they ask a million questions. One of their favorite questions is "Why?" Children love explanations of the world they are discovering. Rudyard Kipling wrote his famous *Just So Stories* for his daughter Effie to explain some of the many questions of a child. How did the camel get its hump? How did the leopard get its spots? How did the elephant get its trunk?

Children also wake up every day with a new thirst for life. "The manna of joy falls in limitless supply, but each day's rations must be gathered afresh." So even though this exercise is for one day, I hope it will be the beginning of obtaining a fresh supply of childlike joy and life each day!

Set aside a time—an hour, several hours, or, if you are able, an entire day—where you give yourself permission to become as a child. *Choose one of these two options*:

1. Let yourself respond to joyful things as a child would. For the amount of time you choose (an hour, several hours, a day), in your reactions when joyful things happen, say to yourself, "If I were a child, I would _____." For example, let's say you get an email from a friend inviting you to go out for coffee. If you were a child, you might gleefully jump up and down in anticipation of being with your friend. So let yourself actually jump up and down. I promise you it will fill you with life. There's no need to be silly, just be joyful to wake up some of the expressions that will bring life to your day. And your joy will be more full-orbed because you included your physical body, rather than just allowing cerebral joy.

2. Let yourself ask questions. Again, choose how long you want to do this exercise. Especially ask "why" questions. Have a continual dialogue with Jesus throughout this time, asking him questions. Let your heart soar with wonder as a little child. You will come alive in places that may be squelched. You don't have to hear an answer. Jesus might even give you a further question, like "Where were you when I made the ostrich's feathers?" Just let yourself wonder *with* God. "Jesus, why do I say the same things my mother or father said?" "Jesus, how does my mouth know to be dry when I'm thirsty?" "Jesus, what is time?" "Jesus, do angels sleep?" These examples are to give you ideas, to turn on the faucet of your own imagination. There's no real form to a good question. Let the wonderer inside of you have free rein to ask any kind of question of Jesus that you desire.

Write in your journal about your experiences of living life as a child for a day. Notice how it felt and what it awakened within you.

eight

YOU HAVE BEEN MADE HOLY

When I was a student in college, Richard J. Foster was my professor. Richard taught me about the deeper life with God and about the spiritual disciplines. I looked up to and admired Richard more than anyone. I asked him if he would baptize me, and he agreed. One afternoon after classes, he and I went to a creek out in the country. It was a dark, overcast day. We sat by the bank of the creek, read Scriptures, and prayed. Then we waded into the water and I knelt down as he said, "I baptize you in the name of the Father, the Son, and the Holy Spirit." He then laid me into the water, covering my head, and I stayed under the water for a few seconds. When I came up out of the water, I was symbolically raised with Christ to brand new life. It was a sacred moment in my life.

What happened next seemed like it was straight out of a movie. As we stood there in the water, the clouds parted, and the sun shone right down on us. As we walked to the bank, Richard noticed that the tree under which we had sat talking was a hawthorn tree. It has branches with long, spiky thorns, reminiscent of the crown of thorns Jesus wore at his crucifixion. Richard walked over and broke off a branch, about a foot long, and gave it to me. He talked about how the Christian life involves suffering, but that it can be a means of growth and transformation.

I kept the branch, as you can imagine. Eventually I put it in what I assumed was a safe place: the top of a tall bookshelf, with the thorns barely visible hanging over the edge. One year for my wife's birthday I bought her a full house cleaning (not a romantic gift, but one she loved). When I came home at the end of the day, the cleaning manager said, "I am very sorry sir, but we broke something. We really hope it is not important."

"Oh, okay," I said. "What happened?"

"When we dusted on top of a bookshelf, an old tree branch fell off and broke in two."

My heart sank.

I went to my office and saw the damage. I gently took the two pieces and placed them in a special container. I was so sad, and so angry with myself for not protecting it better. I resolved that it would never happen again, and it hasn't. I have kept it safe. But a question worth asking is this: Why is it so important to me? That branch is *sacred* to me. It represents a profound moment in my life, a time when I felt God working in me and around me in a deep way. On one level, it is simply an ordinary, small branch from a tree, from a tree out in the country no one may have ever noticed, an otherwise meaningless piece of wood, but not to me. It is sacred to me. It is valuable to me. And I care for and protect it as if it were worth thousands of dollars. Because it is worth that, and much more, to me.

FALSE NARRATIVE: I AM JUST A SINNER, SAVED BY GRACE

When we think about our identity, we often focus on the negative. Most people can tell you with great accuracy all of their shortcomings, the things they do not like, or even despise, about themselves: "I hate my nose," or "I have no willpower," or "I am so stupid."

Perhaps the years of accumulated criticism leave us feeling worthless and no good.

When it comes to our identity as Christians, there are many who will tell you that you are "just a sinner" or "rotten and depraved," but thankfully God, through Jesus, has saved you. Some people believe it is right, even spiritually necessary, to think badly about oneself. They have been led to believe it is godly to dwell on their sinfulness. I have come to believe that not only is this not true, but it is a false narrative with harmful consequences.

I once saw a man wearing a bright blue T-shirt with bold white letters that said, "I am just an old sinner, saved by grace." I asked him about it and he was eager to tell me; I think his T-shirt was an evangelism tool. He smiled and said, "Well, all of us are sinners. There is none righteous, Paul said, no not one—Romans 3:10. But God died for us sinners, and we are saved by grace—it's a gift from God, and not because of our works. This shirt reminds me that I am just a sinner, always a sinner, but I am saved by grace so that I can go to heaven when I die." He then asked if I was saved, and I told him I was. He smiled and said, "Good for you, young man."

At the time, I did not have any retort or rebuttal. That was how I understood the gospel message at that time myself. I even, for a moment, wondered where I could get a T-shirt like his. Something feels right about this narrative: it provides an explanation for why we sin—we are sinners, and sinners sin. Sin is normative behavior for sinners. It lets me off the hook and takes the pressure off. Because we are saved not by our works, but by the grace of God.

There are certainly Bible verses one can quote to support this narrative, such as the one the man himself quoted that declares there is no one who is righteous. And that is true. No one can achieve righteousness, no one can keep all of the Law all of the time. We are human beings, fallen and broken, and prone to wander from the God we love; we fail to do the good we want to do, and we do the bad that we do not want to do (Romans 7:14-20). Of all of the Christian doctrines, the doctrine of the sin of humankind is the easiest to prove. Just watch the news. Or pay attention to your own heart.

The narrative "I am just a sinner, saved by grace" is very appealing. When we feel like the author writing in Romans 7, who confesses, "I do not understand my own actions. For I do not do what I want, but I do the very thing I hate" (Romans 7:15), the slogan on the T-shirt seems like a welcome explanation: "I am just a sinner—sin is what I do." And yet, the narrative brings with it a feeling of dissonance.

Do you feel a dissonance with the narrative "I am just a sinner saved by grace"? Journal about how you feel about those words.

Something inside of me is not comfortable with this confession, not because of pride, but because I know I am called to be something else. I sense inside that God has designed me and destined me for holiness. And there are dozens of passages that call me to it.

THE SOUL'S LONGING FOR PURITY

When I was in seminary, I read Søren Kierkegaard's works. My favorite was *Purity of Heart Is to Will One Thing*. I was so inspired to a life of holiness that I told God I was going to "will one thing"—to be "pure of heart." But of course, I failed. I could barely go an hour without my mind wandering and falling back into my usual thought and behavior patterns. During the Christmas break I decided to get serious. I made it my New Year's resolution: I would wear a purple string around my finger as a constant reminder to stay focused on the will of God (think of this as an early version of the WWJD bracelets). I failed, again and again. My father even said to me, "You look really sad and not well. Are you feeling all right?" I told him I was fine.

Thankfully I gave up on this practice after a week and never tried it again. But I did learn something helpful in my defeat: I felt a great deal of guilt and shame, assuming that my failure was a flaw in me. It increased my feelings of being worthless and weak. I was certain God was disappointed in me, at best. I had a longing to be holy, a desire to be pure in heart, but I was lacking the ability to do it.

One thing I learned from this experience that is absolutely true is this: we cannot be holy of our own accord. You and I do not have the ability or the strength to will the good, to be pure in heart or holy on our own. But it is not because we are sinners. It is because we fail to realize that *in Christ we are saints*. Our embodied souls long for purity because we are designed for holiness. You and I do not have the ability to be holy in and of ourselves. But God made us with this longing, and God provided the solution to it. We cannot make ourselves holy, but we have been made *holy* by the grace of God.

TRUE NARRATIVE: BY THE GRACE OF GOD, I HAVE BEEN MADE HOLY

When I discovered the finality of the cross and the reality of the resurrection—that God, in Christ, has forgiven all sins for all time, and that Jesus rose to impart new life to those who believe—difficult teachings in the New Testament regarding holiness suddenly began to make sense. Jesus died to cleanse us and resurrected to fill, or inhabit, us. As a result, as believers we are people in whom Christ dwells and delights. And if this is so, then all of those passages in the New Testament that declare that we have been made holy make perfect sense.

Because this narrative—by the grace of God, I have been made holy—is so foreign to most of us, I had to spend a lot of time studying the New Testament to believe it. My assumption was that even in Christ our identity is as *sinners*, certainly not saints. But after months and months of studying the Bible, it became clear that we must as Christ-followers self-identify as saints.

To begin, look at how many of the Epistles are addressed to saints (italics added):

- To the church of God that is in Corinth, to those who are sanctified in Christ Jesus, called to be *saints*. (1 Corinthians 1:2)
- Paul, an apostle of Christ Jesus by the will of God, to the *saints* who are in Ephesus and are faithful in Christ Jesus. (Ephesians 1:1)
- Paul and Timothy, servants of Christ Jesus, to all the *saints* in Christ Jesus who are in Philippi, with the bishops and deacons. (Philippians 1:1)
- To the *saints* and faithful brothers and sisters in Christ in Colossae. (Colossians 1:2)

What is striking about this is that we will learn, from the letters themselves, that the people being addressed are *not* saints in their behavior. Paul rebukes the Corinthians for their claims of spiritual superiority, for suing one another in courts, for abusing the Lord's Supper, and for sexual misconduct. As theologian Don J. Payne notes, "Paul's Corinthian correspondence particularly reflects the fact that sanctification characterized Christians who were quite immature and, to state it bluntly, an ethical mess!" Clearly, he does not address them as saints because of their behavior—it is because of their identity in Christ.

One key verse that had puzzled me for a long time is found in my favorite epistle, Colossians. There we read: "But now he has reconciled you by Christ's physical body through death to present you *holy* in his sight, *without blemish* and *free from accusation*" (Colossians 1:22 NIV, italics added).

> Can you fathom that you are holy, without blemish, and free from accusation? Ponder this life-giving reality.

How can we be holy in God's sight? I knew that I was far from holy in terms of my behavior. If you asked me, "Are you as holy as Mother Teresa, or as holy as Billy Graham?" I would say, "Heavens, no! I am nowhere near as holy as those two luminaries." And yet, Colossians 1:22 says that you and I are "holy in his sight."

And not only holy, but "without blemish" and "free from accusation." How is this possible? Certainly not by our efforts. I tried the purple string method and couldn't last more than a few hours *trying* to be holy. So in what sense are we holy? And how? The answer is found in the same verse: Christ has reconciled us (the finality of the cross), and Christ has presented us to God as holy, blameless, and free from accusation. We are not holy because of what we have done, but because of what God, in Christ, has done.

This verse is not a one-off or an aberration. It is the consistent teaching of the Epistles in the New Testament that those who follow Christ have, by the grace of God, been made holy. Here is a sample:

- It is because of him that you are in Christ Jesus, who has become for us wisdom from God—that is, our righteousness, holiness and redemption. (1 Corinthians 1:30 NIV)

- You were washed, you were sanctified, you were justified in the name of the Lord Jesus Christ and in the Spirit of our God. (1 Corinthians 6:11)

- And it is by God's will that we have been sanctified through the offering of the body of Jesus Christ once for all. (Hebrews 10:10)

The author of Hebrews is following the same understanding of Paul—namely, that we have been sanctified, and it is by the "offering of the body of Jesus," not our own works. But note that being sanctified is God's will and design, and that being made holy is not temporary but is once for all time. And the author follows up that thought by stating that by the sacrifice of Jesus we have been made "perfect forever."

- For by one sacrifice he has made perfect forever those who are being made holy. (Hebrews 10:14 NIV)

Again, it is clear from our experience that none of us is perfect in our actions. We have been "made perfect" by the work of God. This is something you and I can never accomplish. Thanks be to God, it is something Jesus accomplished for us.

RELATIONAL SANCTIFICATION

Some have looked at these verses and declarations of our being holy or righteous and mistakenly referred to this as "positional holiness." By this they mean that God has simply put the label "holy" on us—we have moved from one position (unholy, sinful) to another position (holy). The idea here is that Jesus has changed our outer identity, but not our inner character. This is the sentiment of the man in the T-shirt: "I am still a mess, but Jesus has declared me righteous."

I believe this sanctification, this holiness we receive by grace, is not merely positional but is "accomplished," as Don J. Payne describes in his excellent book *Already Sanctified*. And what is it that Jesus accomplished? He cleansed us and regenerated us, and he is now living in and through us. This was accomplished, it was completed—it is not still in process. It happened in and through the work of the Trinity, long before you and I were born. Jesus died for my sins before I committed even one. Jesus rose from the grave to offer me new life before I knew I needed it. He did it all; I did nothing to merit this. But upon my confession of faith and new birth, Christ is now my life (Colossians 3:4). I no longer live, but Christ lives in me (Galatians 2:20).

Sanctification is accomplished by God. Our growth into maturity, which I will address later in this chapter, is a cooperative work between us and God; growing in grace is synergistic. But our holiness is something only God can and did accomplish for us. It is not in us, but in Jesus who lives in us. Our holiness is deeply relational in nature. Theologian Doug Moo puts it this way: "The Christian is not just called to do right in a vacuum but to do right out of a new and powerful relationship that has already been established."

> Our holiness received by grace has been accomplished, and it is not in us but in Jesus who lives in us. What do these words mean to you?

Dallas Willard used a humorous analogy to expose the futility of positional holiness—the barcode found on items at the grocery story. When we check out, the checker scans the barcode, and what registers on the screen is what the barcode says, not necessarily the contents of the package. For example, it may scan as a can of corn, when it is actually a can of beans. All that matters is what the barcode says. This is like those who assume they are made righteous by Jesus' work— the content of their character is irrelevant. But this stands against the call to be conformed to the image of Christ. The change God works in us is not merely a new label, it is an ontological change. *Ontology* means "the nature of being." Our nature is actually changed when we are in Christ. Something is truly different within us, even if our character does not yet match it.

> Our label and our nature change when we are in Christ, though character change takes more time. How have you experienced a change in your nature since you became sanctified?

Far more is happening than just putting a new label on us. Identity is relational, determined by who we are identified with: "For as in Adam all die, so in Christ all will be made alive" (1 Corinthians 15:22 NIV). We were in Adam, we are now in Christ. "For once you were darkness, but now in the Lord you are light. Live as children of light" (Ephesians 5:8). We were darkness, we are now light. Therefore, "walk in the light as he himself is in the light" (1 John 1:7). The relationship determines and directs the behavior. If it is just a label, there is no motivating power for ethical change.

> How does your relationship with Christ determine and direct your behavior?

One of the chief criticisms of the theological teaching that we have been made holy by Christ is that we are not holy in our lives. So what does it matter? Isn't it enough just to pass the checkout line and have the barcode read "holy" when we are, in fact, unholy in our behavior? No. The New Testament teaching on our identity in Christ is this: our identity (the indicative—what we are) leads to and makes possible new behavior (the imperative—what we must do).

WHAT CHRIST HAS DONE

The change wrought by Christ was discussed in chapters six and seven: We have been cleansed by the cross (2 Peter 1:9), and we have been made all-new creations by the resurrection (2 Corinthians 5:17). Jesus is both the source and the motivation for our growth and transformation. The indwelling Christ—made possible by the finality of the cross—is a powerful motivating force for ethical behavior. Jesus has done for us what we cannot do, and the power of Christ now lives in us. What Christ has done compels us to what we can and now must do. There is both an actual holiness (Christ in us) and an aspirational holiness (being conformed to the Christ-form within us).

> Write this down in a visible place so that you can see it every day: "Jesus is both the source and the motivation for our growth and transformation."

The best example of this is found in the sixth chapter of Romans. In chapter five, Paul states that "where sin increased, grace abounded all the more" (Romans 5:20). In other words, you cannot "out-sin" grace. This naturally led to Paul's next question (which he no doubt had been asked), "What then are we to say? Should we continue in sin in order that grace may abound?" (Romans 6:1). It is a fair question: *Can we sin all we want? Grace is going to cover all of our sins, so why not sin as much as we like?* The answer Paul gives is not ethical, but ontological—it is about who we are. Sin is not something fitting for our new nature in Christ. This is his argument:

1. Do you not know that all of us who have been baptized into Christ Jesus were baptized into his death? (Romans 6:3)
2. So you also must consider yourselves dead to sin and alive to God in Christ Jesus. (Romans 6:11)
3. Therefore, do not let sin exercise dominion in your mortal bodies, to make you obey their passions. (Romans 6:12)

The logic is clear: you have died with Christ and risen with Christ—you are in Christ Jesus. Therefore, do not let sin rule you. It does not belong with your new identity.

Notice that Paul does not say, "You can no longer sin." In fact, the discussion implies that Christians *can* sin (and do). Paul's revolutionary teaching is not that we shouldn't sin, but that sin is not fitting with our new nature. Sin is

> Rewrite in your own words Paul's three-step logic for why sin is not fitting with our new nature.

destructive in nature. We don't sin and think, *Wow, that was great! I am so much better for having sinned.* At most, we make excuses for it, but we know it is not good for us. It is not good for a non-believer either. But for a person indwelt by Christ, sin is a complete desecration, an act of vandalism on our sacred nature.

In Corinth, one of the questions among the new converts to the faith was, "Can we continue to engage in temple prostitution?" This question sounds absurd to us, but in Corinth in that day the Gentiles engaged in a kind of religious sexuality. Men would go to the pagan temple, offer a gift of money to the gods, and have sex with temple prostitutes. It was also a part of fertility rituals. So they wanted to know from Paul, "Can we keep doing this?" Paul's answer: "Do you not know that your bodies are members of Christ himself? Shall I then take the members of Christ and unite them with a prostitute? Never!" (1 Corinthians 6:15 NIV). Once again his answer is based on an indicative relationship: Christ is in your body; therefore, the answer is no. He does not say, "No, God is against this practice." He says, "No, it is not fitting with who you are."

> Ponder "God is against this practice" versus "This practice is not fitting with who you are." How could looking at moral choices in this way change the way you live?

I find the words *indicative* and *imperative* helpful here. Indicative refers to what we actually are, and imperative refers to what we ought to do. The imperative, the call to *be* holy, is the natural outflow of the indicative, the fact that we *are* holy. Fleming Rutledge says it well: "The imperative is not only *dependent upon* but *organically produced by* the indicative, or declarative, proclamation." Our growth in holiness is organic, it is natural. Sin, while appealing, is never natural in the Christ-follower. And growth in Christlikeness, while not completed, is the natural *telos*, or "end," for one in whom Christ dwells and delights. Christ has cleansed us and filled us, for that very purpose. Each day I endeavor to remember who I am: *Jim, in whom Christ dwells and delights.* Just being reminded of this reality is inspiring and makes me want to live into my true identity in all I think and do and say.

> Indicative refers to what we actually are, and imperative refers to what we ought to do. The imperative, the call to *be* holy, is the natural outflow of the indicative, the fact that we *are* holy.

CONSONANCE WITH THE CHRIST-FORM

This purpose is perfectly designed and built into the Christ-form of our souls. When I live into the truth that I have been made holy by Christ—not of my own making but by his—there is *consonance* in my embodied soul. When I discovered that by God's grace I had been made holy in Christ, I felt tremendous release. I had felt like a fraud, claiming to be a Christian but inside feeling like I was not living as one. I began to live into the truth of who I am. The lies of the enemy—*How dare you call yourself a Christian!*—began to fade as the voice of the Spirit began to take precedence—"You are God's wanted, desired, beloved, forgiven, alive, and holy child, not based on what you have done but on what God has done."

And at the same time, I found a renewed strength to say no to temptation and sin. Believing that sin was desirable brought *dissonance*, while living into the truth that I am holy brought *consonance*. I was no longer "a sinner saved by grace" but "a saint made holy by Jesus"—that became my identity. Because, as Don Payne describes it, "to live in contradiction to that identity violates something essential. Living at cross-purposes with that identity actually creates dissonance."

I think this truth is also essential in Christian spiritual formation. The lurking danger in Christian formation is legalism. The spiritual disciplines can easily become merit badges to earn God's favor. But if I have been made holy by Christ, the disciplines cannot throw me back on myself. The disciplines for the spiritual life create space for more grace, to empower the already-present Christ-form in me to become more and more alive.

The other lurking danger in Christian spiritual formation, in my view, is the tendency to navel gaze. Formation folks are often contemplative and tend to isolate from others. We are also people who are easily enamored with personality types. I have dear Christian friends who spend more time studying personality types than the Bible, and who define themselves more by their type than by Jesus. This is not to say personality systems cannot be helpful. They certainly can be—for me the Enneagram has been beneficial in leading me to repentance. But these can also become an excuse for our failings.

THE PRIDE-FORM AND GRACE

In a chapter on holiness, it is important to say a word about sin. Fr. Adrian van Kaam's understanding of sin has helped me immensely. He locates our tendency to sin in what he calls the "pride-form." In addition to the Christ-form of our souls, we are also born with a tendency toward self-sufficiency and independence. This is often referred to as *original sin*. It is a kind of interloper in our souls, but a real one. Fr. Adrian uses a great word to describe it: *autarkic*. It is a desire for self-rule, a desire to be in control, a desire to be God.

The autarkic pride-form is the "original source of paranoid fears, excessive pleasure seeking, and anxious, overprotective, depreciative dispositions." As much as we long for God, for the "more than" in life, we are easily led to eat the forbidden fruit that promises we can be our own god; the pride-form resists grace. Adam and Eve had no need, no lack, and no want. But within them, and within me, is something that shuts down the embodied soul's need for connection, for true consonance, and settles for the faux connection found in most sins. The pride-form bottles up the life-giving sources of our soul in the pursuit of personal gratification.

But grace kills the pride-form: "The grace of God always kills before it makes alive," wrote the great theologian T. F. Torrance. Grace can only be received in a state of humility—the pride-form is a clenched fist; humility is an open hand. "The grace of rescue from the treachery of the pride-form is available to every Christian," write Rebecca Letterman and Susan Muto. The pride-form will always create dissonance, and is thus always at war with our embodied souls. Ultimately, for the Christian, "attaining a sense of self-worth means experiencing myself as fallible and frail, yet capable with God's grace of transcending my frailty." I am more sinful than I can imagine and I am more deeply loved than I can possibly hope. Love prevails, and when it does it is well with my soul.

And grace is the power that not only makes us holy but transforms us into Christlikeness. Many assume that grace is opposed to effort, that grace is paralyzed by any work on our part. In truth, more Christians are paralyzed by grace than saved by it. Dallas Willard writes, "Grace is not opposed to effort, it is opposed to earning. Earning is an attitude. Effort is an action." Our sanctity in Christ must not inhibit our efforts to grow in holiness, but rather should inspire it. The Holy Spirit will never allow for passivity. As George MacDonald wrote,

"Earning is an attitude. Effort is an action." Give examples of these stances in relation to grace.

> Love loves unto purity. Love has ever in view the absolute love-
> liness of that which it beholds. Therefore all that is not beautiful
> in the beloved, all that comes between and is not of love's kind,
> must be destroyed. And our God is a consuming fire.

Love is what made us holy, and Love is what is making us holy.

APPROACHING THE THRONE OF GRACE
WITH CONFIDENCE

The thorn branch I wrote about at the beginning of this chapter now sits in a special place in my office. It is there because I love it. I keep it near me because it is sacred and valuable. Nearby sits one of my favorite photos. It is of John F. Kennedy Jr., the son of the late President Kennedy. It is a photo of him as a small boy, sitting in his father's desk in the Oval Office in the White House. I love it because he is playing and he wants to be near his father, and his father wants to have him near.

What is striking about this picture is that it is taken in the office of the most powerful person in the world. You and I cannot just walk into the Oval Office, but this little boy could. Why? Because of who he was in relation to the one in power. This is a great illustration of those of us who are in Christ. We are God's children, and the Spirit within compels us to cry, "Abba!" And God welcomes us, because

God, in Christ, desires us, loves us, forgives us, lives in us, and has made us holy. This is why the author of Hebrews encourages us, "Let us therefore approach the throne of grace with boldness, so that we may receive mercy and find grace to help in time of need" (Hebrews 4:16). And it is why Paul tells the Ephesians, "In him and through faith in him we may approach God with freedom and confidence" (Ephesians 3:12 NIV).

Say this aloud: "I am loved by God without condition, I have been forgiven forever, and I have been made holy. I can approach God with freedom and confidence."

Say this right now: "I was wanted by God before I existed. I am loved by God without condition. I have been forgiven forever, I have been made alive, and I have been made holy by the grace of God in Jesus. And I can approach God with freedom and confidence." Try saying this for a week and see what it does to your soul.

That is the word of truth. It is not the word of this author, but of the Author of all things. Believe it. Trust in it. And sing and dance in the kingdom of God's beloved Son.

say yes to god always

"But God proves his love for us in that while we still were sinners Christ died for us" (Romans 5:8), but God's love does not leave us in our unholy state. God's life sanctifies us, or "holy-fies" us.

The life of the believer is exciting as we connect with and live out of the life of Christ that lives in us. Christ sanctifies our entire being when he dwells within us. Not in external ways, like behavior modification, but in our deepest places where our very nature is transformed. Godly behavior is the fruit of our holiness, not the root of it. It's like the Psalm 1 tree that is planted by living waters, soaking up all that life so it can produce leaves and fruit. It would be hard for a tree to produce leaves and fruit without drawing from its source of life.

So how do we draw from our source of life to produce the fruit of holiness that is consonant with the Christ-form within us?

Daily life includes many calls to relinquish our pride (that is, our independent will that wants to be in charge) to God's ways. Adrian van Kaam says that God speaks in the midst of everydayness.

Here and now is where we must listen to life and say yes to the whispered appeals from God in our real lives. Yes to God sounds easy when a healthy child arrives. Our first job. A new home. A splendid vacation. A striking sunset. But a crisis brings dissonance and disruption. We can respond either with a sense of abandonment by God, or with trust. We often hang in help-lessness between the two. Have we been abandoned by the Mystery? Or can we abandon ourselves to the Mystery?

Is there a call in your life right now to relinquish your will and live in consonance with Christ in you? If so, the call is to choose what is best, not what is worst.

Relinquishment requires humility, a yielding of our will to God, a trust that God's ways are the most good and beautiful of all. God's grace will empower you by killing the pride-form first, setting you free to live in consonance with wholeness.

Faced with crisis, Job expressed his feelings of abandonment—"Why do you hide your face, and count me as your enemy?" he cried (Job 13:24). But God gave Job the grace to relinquish his will and to abandon himself to God. Job made a soul-stirring confession of great hope:

> For I know that my Redeemer lives,
>   and at the last he will stand upon the earth.
> And after my skin has been thus destroyed,
>   yet in my flesh I shall see God,
> whom I shall see for myself,
>   and my eyes shall behold, and not another. (Job 19:25-27 ESV)

Job's story is long and winding, but God's grace enables Job to say yes to God with complete abandonment. Job would end up placing his hand over his mouth, signifying he would no longer question God's ways.

Abraham is a great example of relinquishment flowing out of his relationship with God. Abraham did not offer up Isaac out of a vac-uum but after years of receiving God's love and care, of believing God's dreams for him were bigger and better than his own for him-self. Out of deep love and trust did Abraham sacrifice the dream of having his own son. Relinquishment opened the floodgates of bless-ings as numerous as the stars.

Imagine what saying yes to God always could look like in your life. There is a relational context to holiness. You do what is right as a stream flows out of a spring, in an organic way, flowing out of your relationship with Christ who dwells in and delights in you.

1. Spend some time alone with God. Ask him what the next step is for you to live in consonance with Christ in you, the hope of glory. Then listen to God.

2. Write what you hear God saying in your journal. Maybe it's something small. Maybe it's something big. The size isn't important; the direction is. Job blessed God with his mouth long before he yielded and trusted God with his whole being over his huge losses of family and possessions. Both were growth.

3. This isn't something to rush. For now, just connect with the indwelling Christ. Ask him for his heart about your situation. Simply draw from your source of life. Notice the graces that Jesus is already giving to help you.

4. Finally, in your journal write the graces that God has already given you that might help you say yes to God.

nine

you have a sacred story

Readers of my other books may be aware that our second child, Madeline, was born with a chromosomal disorder that shortened her lifespan. She died not long after her second birthday. After Madeline died, my wife Meghan and I spent a lot of time healing. One day Meghan said to me with a smile, "I'm pregnant." It was a moment of great joy and great terror. We knew we wanted to have another child, but after what had happened with Madeline, we were scared. We spent the first eight months of the pregnancy on pins and needles. Every doctor's appointment became an event in which we held our breath. Throughout the pregnancy, everything was fine.

Then, in the final month—the same point at which we found out that there were grave health issues with Madeline—the doctor scheduled us to have one last sonogram. The technician who performed the sonogram did not know our story. But she kept saying, "It all looks great—perfect hands, perfect feet, heart looks perfect." We loved hearing this. "Everything looks absolutely perfect."

Then she said, "I can also tell the gender. Do you know, or would you like to know?" she asked.

We did not know up to that point, but we did want to know, so we said, "Yes."

"It's a baby girl," she said.

Meghan and I looked at each other in amazement.

"Have you chosen a name?" she asked.

Meghan and I looked at each other again, and without missing a beat we said the same name at the exact same time. And, most surprisingly, it was a name neither of us had ever discussed or even suggested.

In unison we said, "Hope."

For the next few years, as Hope grew and developed into a bright, vibrant, lively, sunny, blonde-haired, happy little girl, we beamed with joy. Hope—which means "certainty in a good future"—had become a living example of the theological virtue after which she had been named. And everyone who knew her—friends, parents, teachers—all said the same thing: "She sure lives up to her name; she is so positive and joyful, and full of . . . hope." That became a running joke in our family.

Caveat: I want you, reader, to know that Hope's story that follows is shared not only with her permission but with her hope that it may be of help to others. As her father, it is a hard story to tell. But, along with Hope, I share it because I know that we all struggle with parts of our own stories, events we wish had never happened but that God has allowed to happen. It is by grace that we can find meaning and healing through Christ.

When Hope turned fifteen, we noticed she seemed to be carrying a burden. The light in her soul had dimmed. She shared with Meghan and me that she had been experiencing a great deal of anxiety. We asked her if she wanted to see someone, perhaps a counselor, for help. She said yes. We found a good and trusted therapist, a young woman of faith and kindness, and Hope shared with us that she was benefiting from the therapy sessions. Little by little we saw Hope beginning to heal. But we had no idea what she had been dealing with.

Then we got a call from her counselor. She said, "Hope would like for both of you to come in and meet with me. There are some things she wants you to know about, but she would rather have me tell you than tell you herself."

We were stunned. But we were happy to meet with the counselor. When we got to her office we sat down on a couch. She shared how much she loved Hope and how wonderful Hope is, and we thanked her and agreed. Then she said, "Hope has been carrying a terrible burden."

"Please tell us," I asked.

"When Hope was thirteen she was physically and sexually assaulted by a boy at her school. She kept it to herself. She even hid a bruise the boy gave her. She confided in two of her friends, but they did not believe her. And then they abandoned her, and eventually even betrayed her and bullied her," the counselor explained.

The air was sucked out of our lungs, as if we had been kicked in the stomach. We were in shock, because we had no idea.

"Hope was good at hiding all of this from you," she said.

"But why?" Meghan asked. "Why would she not tell us?"

"Because . . ." the therapist started to answer, but got choked up, as did we. *"Because of her name.* She is ashamed of what happened to her. She knows that she came into a broken family, a family that lost a child. She loved her name when she was young, but after the assault and the bullying, she felt she was broken, that she was no longer able to *be the hope* that you, and everyone, needed her to be."

YOU HAVE A STORY

Each of us is conceived at a particular time and born into a specific family and communal setting. We had literally nothing to do with this. It happened to us. We all have a birth date. We are born into a body we did not choose and given a name we did not choose. We are all born in a place, time, and culture. We all have a biological father and mother (even if they only provided sperm and egg). Someone or a group of people raised us—as infant humans we are completely helpless and must be fed and cared for. This is all a part of your story. It is what Dallas Willard calls your "circle of origin." It has a great deal to do with who you are, and who you will forever be. We all have a story to tell.

There are many possibilities for our stories. Perhaps we:

- were a first child, a middle child, or the baby in our family;
- were an only child, or one of many children;
- were adopted;
- had parents who stayed married, or we grew up in a divorced home;
- had parents or caregivers who were loving, or perhaps they were abusive;
- had a parent who died when we were young or a teenager;
- were born into poverty, or wealth, or the middle class;
- went to public school, or private school;
- are Black, or Brown, or White, or another ethnicity or skin color;
- were born and raised in the United States, Europe, East Asia, Africa, the Middle East, or South America;
- were neglected or abused; or
- had many or few friends.

These are all a part of our circle of origin. They have shaped us, for good or for ill. Our familial, cultural, historical, and social dimensions have formed us, even without our awareness. There are many things that form us, but one of the most essential is the sociohistorical dimension. It plays a markedly formative role in our lives. We are blessed, or burdened, by the story we find ourselves in, by the sins and the graces of our family. We are not only shaped by our parents, but also our grandparents, and their parents and grandparents before them—even if we never met them. As Rainer Maria Rilke notes, "They who passed away long ago, still exist in us, as predisposition, as burden upon our fate, as murmuring blood, and as gesture that rises up from the depths of time."

Our circle of origin and our personal relationships are of enormous importance for the formation of our spirit and our entire life. Mom and Dad not only give us their DNA, they also give us our sense of worth. I not only have "my father's eyes," but I carry in myself how he looked at me with his eyes, and both are equally determinative of how I see myself. Our inner world of thoughts and feelings is formed in part by what others say about us and do to us.

The question we are born asking is this: *Am I wanted?* We all have an innate longing for rootedness. We long for the assurance that someone is for us. We long

> What is your sociohistorical story, your circle of origin?

for a "circle of sufficiency." And we seek this sufficiency from our circle of origin. "Did Mom and Dad really want me?" "Do they really love me?" are inescapable questions that matter deeply. Our circle of sufficiency widens to our siblings, then to extended family. Grandparents or aunts and uncles have raised many people, but the question remains the same: "Is there someone who is for me?" The "forness" must be there or we suffer, and ultimately there is only one truly sufficient circle—the Trinity. The great John of Kronstadt is known to have said, "When you are dejected, remember this, that God the Trinity looks upon you with eyes brighter than the sun."

Apart from the Trinity, all of our circles of sufficiency are ultimately insufficient. That is because they are dependent on fallen, broken, limited, and finite humans. In the kingdom of this world, there are no completely sufficient circles. Even the best of parents, siblings, friends, and others in social circles are bound to harm us. They may or may not intend to, but it is inevitable. The kingdom of this world is a culture of rejection. And that rejection comes in two main forms: assault or withdrawal.

Assault is aggressive and withdrawal is passive, but both are harmful. "We assault others," Dallas Willard writes, "when we act against what is good for them and cause harm or pain. We

withdraw from someone when we regard their well-being as matters of indifference." Aggressive assault can be verbal or physical.
And it comes in varying levels of severity, and causes varying levels
of trauma. Physical attack and violence are common in our world.
My sister, Vicki, has worked many years for the Child Abuse Prevention program in her city. She hears and sees the evidence
of children being physically and sexually harmed. These kinds of
assaults, sadly, typically come from within families and create scars
hat last lifetimes.

Withdrawal is a form of social evil that is subtle, but causes great
harm. If assault is an active form of harm, withdrawal is felt in the
absences, the lack of interest, the neglect, the unspoken sense that
we do not matter. It is seen in not getting picked, being overlooked or
passed over. In some ways, withdrawal can be more painful than assault. In situations of assault, there is a sense that we are a threat to
someone. In situations of withdrawal, we are treated as though we do
not matter at all. Whether someone says or does something hurtful
to us, or whether they say or do nothing at all, the message is the
same: no one is *for us.*

If we experience a deep sense of welcome, love, reception, and
value in our early years by our parents and siblings, it will likely create a sense of rootedness that will enable us to withstand the many
forms of rejection we will experience in our lifetimes. And we will
experience rejections; they come in active and passive, direct and
indirect, forms each day. They shape the story we find ourselves in.
But it is not only the story we find ourselves in that shapes us, it is
also how we narrate the story. A million little things have happened
to you, and you have shaped them into a story. There is our actual
story, and there is also our perception of that story.

The question is: *Is the story we are telling about ourselves* true
or false?

FALSE NARRATIVES: I AM WHAT OTHERS HAVE DONE TO ME AND MY PAST HAS NOTHING TO DO WITH ME

There are two false narratives that are common when it comes to the impact of the social and historical dimension of our lives. The first narrative develops when we "ultimize" (make ultimate or most important) the parts of our story; the second emerges when we minimize or deny our story.

The first false narrative gives too much power to our stories, to the things that have happened to us—the assaults and withdrawals. It develops when we *ultimize* our story by believing that our story (real or perceived) is all that we are. Believing that we are our story and that our story is us, we make our sociohistorical narrative ultimate—we allow it to define us. We begin to believe that we are the things that have happened to us, the things people have said about us, and the things we have done in response. We ultimize our story when we think, *I am my story,* rather than *I have a story.*

Can you name a part of your story that you have "ultimized"?

The second false narrative gives too little power to our stories, when we try to escape our stories or play down their role in our formation. This common error we can make is to *minimize* our story. Sometimes the things that have happened to us are too painful for us to face, or sometimes we deny their effect on us. I have come to believe that God graciously allows us not to have to face all of our brokenness in its fullness; to do so might destroy us.

Can you name a part of your story that you have minimized?

A friend of mine spent many years denying the impact of a stepmother who abused her verbally whenever her father was not around. On one occasion she tried to tell her father about the abuse, but her father did not believe her. The pain was so deep that she could not face it. Unconsciously, she began doing everything in her power to please her father to make up for the deficit she felt; perfectionism was a way of soothing her pain.

It was not until she was in her forties that she experienced a transcendence crisis that led her to seek help. She had lived for over three decades in a kind of denial about her childhood pain. Her therapy allowed her to explore the impact of her circle of insufficiency. Her relationship with Jesus would also play a large part in her healing. She told me, "For years, if someone asked about my parents or my upbringing, I would tell people I had a great home life, and that my parents were great. I just didn't want to face how it all affected me. The pain was too great. But at a certain point, I could no longer live with it or the pain I was causing others."

There is a Jesuit maxim that says, "Give me a boy until he is seven, and I will give you the man." A British documentary, 56 Up, tried to see if that maxim contained any truth. In 1964, director Michael Apted began filming the lives of eight children who were all seven years old. He then filmed the same children seven more times, every seven years, until they reached the age of fifty-six. The maxim proved largely true. The different socioeconomic, religious, and familial dimensions of each of these seven-year-old kids were determinative of much of their adult behavior. The kids from broken homes, for example, spent much of their lives trying to create stable families for their children, searching for it but often failing at it.

Columnist and author David Brooks notes,

> We are the beneficiaries of our ancestors. The dead show up in our lives. We are formed by the places we grew up in. When we form our identity, we are telling a story about ourselves. And the story is the emerging of all the things we understand and don't understand. And that story then becomes our identity, and it becomes the way we see the world. And if you change the story you tell about yourself, you can change the way you see the world.

Our families and cultures, our parents and teachers and friends, shape us a great deal. But we are not our stories—we are something more, something far greater and more wonderful than the things that people have done or said to us. As Van Kaam writes, "It is a lifelong task of formation to help people become the *subject* instead of only the *object* of their history." We are not what has happened to us, but what has happened to us matters. However, we are the subjects of a much better story than the one most of us are telling ourselves.

In his book *A Grace Disguised*, Gerald Sittser tells the story of how he lost three generations of his family—his mother, his wife, and his daughter—on a lonely Idaho road in a tragic auto accident. "The experience of loss," he explains, "does not have to be the defining moment of our lives. Instead, the defining moment can be *our response* to the loss. It is not what happens *to* us so much as what happened *in* us." This in no way assuages the pain and the grief of our losses. Dr. Sittser is stating the truth that it is not only what happens to us, but more so our response to what happens *to* us that matters. It is what God can do *in* us that makes healing possible.

TRUE NARRATIVE: I HAVE A UNIQUE, GOD-ORDAINED STORY

For many of us, our stories produce either gratitude or shame. We can be glad, for example, that we had good parents, that we lived relatively pain-free lives. Or we can feel shame for what has happened to us, for the neglect as well as the assaults that we have endured. But we, as well as our parents, family, and friends, are not the authors of our story. The author of our story is God.

You are not merely a story. You are an unceasing spiritual being, a divinely designed gift from God. You are not a story, but you *have* a story and that story matters. If you neither ultimize nor minimize your story, you can see your story in the right light. And the only person who can tell your story and mine is Jesus. And his word to us goes something like this:

You were uniquely incarnated into a specific family, culture, and time. God planned it for you; you cannot change this. It has a large influence on you, but it does not define or limit you. It has not only happened to you, it has happened for you. The sooner you embrace this dimension of who you are, the sooner you can become who you were created to be. This is your story.

You have a family, but you are not your family. You were raised in a culture and time and it has shaped you, but you are not merely a product of them. What has happened to you has influenced you and shaped you in deeper ways than any of us can know, but you are not defined or limited by them.

Does this narrative cause you comfort or distress? Reflect on why you might be feeling this way.

For many this narrative is comforting; for others it causes great distress. And it may be a source of contention for those who push back, saying, "How could a good God have allowed me to be harmed or abused or neglected?" That is a fair and legitimate question. The step from God *allowed* to God *caused* is a short one, and one that is easy to make. If God is all powerful, and all good but bad things have happened to me, then God is either not all powerful or not all good, or so it seems and feels. I understand, I relate to, and I sympathize with this position.

I believe that God can, and desires to, use what has happened to us for an ultimate good, though perhaps we will not know it in this life. Paul boldly claims, "And we know that in all things God works for the good of those who love him, who have been called according to his purpose" (Romans 8:28 NIV). I know that God has worked a lot of good out of the death of our daughter Madeline. But in truth, there is much I do not understand.

Our stories are so vast, I believe, it will take thousands of years to fully comprehend the complexity of our historical and social influences. Susan Muto and Rebecca Letterman explain how our families, cultures, and communities form a massive matrix which "bestows on us rich historical resources of formative wisdom that extend far beyond what would be possible for one person to attain." Our stories are vast, and far beyond our comprehension. But ultimately, we are God's stories, not our own. And our healing and our growth potential come when we turn to God and allow God to write us into a larger, more beautiful story.

HEALING YOUR STORY

Our story is really not our story. It started long before we were born, in the mind of God. That truth, that reality, does not minimize the pain we feel. Losses, rejection, neglect, verbal and physical assault affect us—but they do not get the last word. Our circles of origin form us in ways we carry for the rest of our lives. And our circles of sufficiency, no matter how strong, will ultimately fail to provide the deep needs of our soul. That is why true healing comes only from the One who is truly sufficient, the One whose love never fails. As Willard writes, "Love comes to us from God. That must be our unshakable circle of sufficiency."

In order for healing to happen, we have to stop hiding our story by keeping it all to ourselves. Letting others into our pain helps us process what has happened to us. This does not mean we must be an open book before all people with no healthy boundaries, but it does mean that we find trusted people with whom we can share our pains. Shame and guilt grow in the dark of secrecy, but they die in the healing light of trusting relationships.

> When have you seen healing happen in the light among trusting relationships?

Hope's first transcendence crisis happened two years before her therapy, at a Christian camp one summer. She did not want to go because she had, in her words, "lost her faith" after the assault, though we were not aware of that. But a persistent friend talked her into going. While she was there, she began developing close relationships with a few friends she would later call her "camp family." During a worship time she said she "could see the Holy Spirit pouring out of them."

Toward the end of the camp, one of the speakers encouraged the campers to put all their trust in Jesus to help them overcome their fears. The next day they rode on a zipline, and Hope was shaking in fear as she climbed the ladder. When she reached the platform, she prayed, "Jesus, I put all my trust in you. If you are here with me, then take away my fear." The fear vanished, and she leaped off the platform and slid down to the end with a smile. When she got to the end, she said, "I think I am a total Jesus freak."

A few years after her therapy and healing, at that same camp, during some tender times of deep sharing, Hope felt safe enough to talk about her assault with these trusted friends. She shared what had happened to her, the pain she had endured. She was met with understanding, acceptance, and compassion. The Holy Spirit can work through people and, apparently, through ziplines. A new circle of sufficiency had formed through her Christian friends and Jesus himself. What is important to note is that Hope was no longer defining herself by what happened to her, nor denying what happened to her. She was open to letting God create a new story. We must surrender authorship to God. Jesus is not only the author and perfecter of our faith, but also the author and perfecter of our stories.

A few years after sharing her story at camp, Hope felt she would benefit from doing some more therapy work. I asked if she would be interested in doing a similar program to the one I had done—a week-long intensive program. She thought that would be helpful, so I took her to Denver, to Restoring the Soul, where she worked with a therapist, Kelley, who specializes in working with young female survivors of assault.

During the third day of therapy, Kelley asked her if she would be willing to pray and invite Jesus into her story of trauma; Hope agreed. The following is Hope's account of what happened during this time of prayer:

> I felt anxious, but I agreed. In silent prayer, I asked Jesus my question: "Where were you during my assault?" After a few minutes, I felt a lump in my throat and tears in my eyes. I heard a voice in my heart whisper, "I was with you, my dear, but what happened to you was not my doing. And because of your shame, you did not want me there." I wept. I told Kelley what Jesus said, and we talked through the response. Kelley asked my younger self to come forward—the younger self who was in the midst of my trauma. My middle school self said that after the assault, I stopped believing in Jesus. After the assault, the abuse that I was enduring made me question what kind of God would let his precious child go through that. I believe Jesus was telling me that he wanted to be with me, but that I would not let him in because of my shame. While it will take a long time to fully grasp this, it was so freeing to know that *Jesus was there*. He was with me even when I didn't want him to be.

This prayer experience, Hope said, was a breakthrough in her healing journey.

Hope's journey is not over. Indeed, each of our journeys of healing last a lifetime. Van Kaam wisely reminds us, "The reversal of traumas may take a lifetime. The therapy that enables us to cope does not work like magic; it proceeds according to *the pace of grace*. What counts is not so much our success as our striving for wellness with Christ at our side."

A few years later when Hope was in college, she attended a conference I was speaking at along with William Paul Young, the author of *The Shack*, a book that meant a lot to Hope. Paul was kind enough to spend some time with Hope and me and learn about her story. Paul's own story contains many years of pain and abuse, and he has found true healing through the Trinity.

Hope shared the story of how she got her name, and how after her assault and bullying she felt the burden of her name, because, as she said, "I never felt I could be enough." Paul smiled at her, looked right into her eyes, and said, "Hope, you have always been enough."

Brené Brown wrote, "When we have the courage to walk into our story and own it, we get to write the ending." I would modify this slightly: "we get to write the ending, with God's help." We have so little control over our lives. We are not born with a clean slate, but into an ongoing story, one that began long before we were born. We do not pick our parents or the names they give us. And in a sense, even the names our parents give us are not our true names; according to Revelation 2:17, we will one day be given a white stone with a new name given by God written on it.

> What name do you imagine God might have for you on your white stone?

The world we live in is an act of grace. We are only here by an act of grace. The party would not have been the same without us, and beautiful and terrible things will certainly happen to us. But we are never alone. And because of that, we do not need to be afraid. There is only one thing for us to do: receive life as a gift.

Retelling Your sacred story

Sometimes we absorb deep beliefs about who we are from things that happen to us. We may not even be consciously aware of the belief we hold, but as Dallas Willard writes, "We believe something when we act as if it were true." We might not realize what false identity we have formed, but if we act as if it were true, we believe it. Our stories can help us access any wrongly held beliefs about ourselves. Curt Thompson writes:

> You construct your understanding of the world and your place in it through the lens of your own story. And the manner and context in which you reflect on your story (in your mind) or tell your story (to others) become part of the fabric of the narrative itself. In other words, the process of reflecting on and telling others your story, and the way you experience others hearing it, actually shapes the story.

For example, if you experience looks of shame or disapproval on another's face when you tell your story, that will shape how you feel about your story, and it will also alter the way you tell it the next time.

In this chapter two types of harm were addressed: assault, when someone hurts you by an act inflicted upon you; and withdrawal, when something you needed was withheld. Let's briefly look at two simple examples from literature of these types of harm, and then at the re-storying of both examples.

Assault: In *The Lord of the Rings*, the Steward of Gondor has two sons. The Steward loves and admires his older son, Boromir, but disdains his younger son, Faramir. It would be easy for Faramir to believe deep down that he is worthless, because his father continually communicates his low opinion of Faramir, both verbally and in his actions.

Withdrawal: In the fairy tale "Cinderella," her stepmother and stepsisters withhold even the simplest kindnesses from the girl. Cinderella is left to herself, made to stay in the corner of her room far away from the food, fun, and fellowship in the sitting room with the others. Isolation is one of the hardest experiences for a human being to bear, because we are made for loving attachment to others. Cinderella is denied pretty dresses and instead wears rags. Her stepmother does not nurture her or love her as she needs.

Now let's look to your own story. Don't worry if you can't remember certain periods of your childhood or life, that is not uncommon.

Please read through sections one through five below before you actually do the practice of retelling your sacred story.

The divine connection is first in this exercise so that you start with joy and increase your capacity for the rest of the exercise. Refresh your memory with a time when you had a good connection with God, with no pain around the edges—a splinter-free memory. Then examine any harm in your story from a safe, joyful place with God. And if you experience any emotion that feels too intense or too painful, please just return to the divine connection and wait to ask God about the painful story when you are with a trusted counselor or spiritual director.

1. Divine Connection:

   Description: Remember a time when you had a good connection with God. It may have been watching a sunrise or hiking in the woods, or a special time of prayer or worship. When a memory comes, let yourself just enjoy it. Then, notice how your five senses experienced the memory: as you enjoy the memory, what do you see, hear, taste, smell, or touch? Let yourself experience your sense perceptions again. Then, notice how you feel in your body, and describe that in a few words. Next, notice what emotions you are feeling in the memory—describe those in a few words. Finally, how do you perceive God's presence with you in this memory? Enjoy that for a minute or two more.

Directions: Spend five to seven minutes on your divine connection.

- Remember a divine connection to God. Enjoy it for a minute!
- Activate five senses in the memory: see, hear, taste, smell, touch.
- How does your body as a whole feel?
- What emotions are there for you in this memory?
- How do you perceive God's presence in this memory?
- Savor your connection to God in this memory.

2. Remember:

Ask Jesus: Has my perception of myself been shaped by the way others have treated me, either by assault (causing hurt) or by withdrawal (the lack of love, connection, attachment, affirmation)? See what comes up: please try to identify a hurt (assault or withdrawal) that is significant but not too stressful for this exercise. If you have hurts that seem very deep or overwhelming, consider doing this exercise with a trained professional.

Write the assault or withdrawal in your journal, but don't try to dwell on it or relive it.

3. Any False Narratives:

Ask Jesus: Are there any false, deeply held beliefs about myself based on what someone did to me or didn't do for me? Notice what comes up, and write that in your journal. Not all false beliefs are easy to identify, so don't be concerned if you do not immediately think of any.

4. Let Jesus Retell Your Story:

Prayerfully, invite Jesus into your story. Sit with him without hurry. Ask him anything about it that you want to know. Wait upon him. Ask him to redeem your story . . . to re-story it. Notice how *re-story* is very close to *restore*. Jesus may answer you in a still small voice today, or he may unfold his truth gradually. His redemptive power can break connections between the mistreatment and your false belief—how he does that is individual, and Jesus knows what you need. Write in your journal any ways that Jesus heals your false narrative or sense of yourself. Ask him to replace any lies with the truth. Remember that this exercise might need to be repeated more than once, and it might be best done with a trained professional, especially if you are already seeing such a person.

5. Retell Your Story:

If you have done this exercise on your own, now tell your story to a trusted friend, priest, pastor, counselor, or spiritual director. Share the harm done to you, but you do not need to disclose the pain in too much detail. Next share what false belief about yourself you identified that you have been living out of as a result. Tell how Jesus is re-storying the incident that led you to the false belief. Focus on the re-storying that Jesus is doing. Let the listener interact or ask you questions.

PUTTING OFF FALSE IDENTITIES

We are not what has happened to us. Healing is a journey and whether or not you always feel it, the Healer is your constant companion. Jesus is writing your story with you.

Re-storying assault: Faramir struggled with the belief that he had to prove himself to his father, and almost stole the ring of power to do so. But the part of him that knew the truth won. The truth became the bigger story. Faramir eventually rejected the story that his wounds from his father told, and he chose to act in a way that was worthy of love and admiration. Faramir released Frodo and the ring, refusing to let his father's opinion of him define him or cause him to try to earn his father's love by capturing a prize for him.

Re-storying withdrawal: Cinderella was hurt by her isolation, but she befriended mice. She felt dejected when she wasn't allowed to go to the ball, but she dared to dream and in the end became a princess! She broke out of the lies her circle of origin wanted her to believe about herself—and so can you.

Yes, these are stories of fiction, but they are good stories because they are true. Indeed, we are princesses and princes because we are children of the King! Real Faramirs and real Cinderellas do overcome the false narrative that they are what has happened to them. Disapproval, rejection, and isolation don't get the last word in our souls.

> Praise the Lord, my soul;
>> all my inmost being, praise his holy name.
> Praise the Lord, my soul,
>> and forget not all his benefits—
> who forgives all your sins
>> and heals all your diseases,
> who redeems your life from the pit
>> and crowns you with love and compassion,
> who satisfies your desires with good things
>> so that your youth is renewed like the eagle's.
>> (Psalm 103:1-5 NIV)

ten

YOU ARE called

When he was fourteen, E. J. was working on his "God and Country" Scouting award that required he meet with his pastor. After a few meetings, the pastor told him, "You should consider being a minister one day." He felt it was the first of God's whispers in his life in regard to his vocation. He took this seriously into consideration because he loved the church so much. But his family moved to another state and joined a new church, which meant a different minister. According to an aptitude test he took, he learned he was good at science and engineering but also had gifts for ministry. At eighteen he was still trying to discern a call for his life, so E. J. met with his new minister to ask his advice. The pastor said, "If you can do anything other than ministry, do it."

E. J. was stunned by the response—so surprised that he failed to ask the follow-up questions he later wished he had asked, such as, "Are you saying that because you wish *you* hadn't gone into ministry?" or "Are you saying that to make sure I know what I want?" He put a lot of weight in what this minister said, so when it came time to choose a school and a career path, he chose to go to college and pursue a chemical engineering degree. There he met his future wife and after college got a corporate job working in New York City. "I felt good about my career decisions, but I always wondered if I could have impacted more people's lives if I'd gone into ministry," he said. He spent the next thirty-one years working in the corporate world.

His corporate job paid him a lot more money than a church job would have, which enabled him to give generously to the church throughout his life. He volunteered for many roles in the church, working years as the adult sponsor of the youth group and influencing many lives—many of the youth stay in touch with him to this day. He also led a Bible study in his office in New York and influenced his coworkers with his faith and character. At the urging of a friend in his church, he enrolled in a lay-speaking training program and was licensed to preach. He preached in several churches and got a lot of positive feedback. When he led a men's retreat on spiritual formation, he felt a strong urge to do more things like it. When the retreat was over, he thought, *I really love this.*

Then, when E. J. was fifty-four, God sent not a whisper but a lightning bolt. E. J.'s company was downsizing and offered him a generous retirement package if he wanted it. He considered going to seminary and becoming a pastor. When he told his wife, Penny, she said, "I always knew this day would come." So at fifty-four he went to seminary for three years, was ordained, and was the pastor of a church in Connecticut for eight years before retiring at sixty-five. He loved his time working as a pastor, preaching and teaching and leading the congregation. The church was small and struggling when he came, and had grown and was healthy by the time he left. He was there long enough to learn that ministry is not a constant joyful experience and comes with its own challenges; still, he was grateful he got the chance to do it.

I asked him if he regretted not going into ministry as a young man, and he said he had no regrets at all. He loved his job in the corporate world and was grateful for all it helped him do in his life.

"It was a great plan for my life," he said. "And who knows, ministry is difficult, and if I had gone into ministry from the beginning I might have quit at some point." He told me something I found very helpful: "I learned to abandon the false narrative that God's call is like a bull's-eye on a target, that there is something specific God has in mind for each of us, and if you miss it, you are outside of God's will."

He knows now that God whispers to us throughout our lives, offering direction and counsel. He believes God has designed us with many passions and gifts, and that there are many ways we can live out our callings.

FALSE NARRATIVE: YOUR WORK DOESN'T MATTER TO GOD

A very common narrative about our professions is that we are not called to a certain career; we simply choose to do whatever we like doing, what makes us happy, what will make us the most money, or what other people tell us we should do. A large percentage of people simply find their occupations by default: "My parents were teachers, so I grew up around education, so teaching seemed like the right thing for me to do."

Many people end up working in a profession because an opportunity presented itself. "I knew a guy who sold cars, and he told me about an opening," a former student told me. "So I applied and got it. I don't really like it, but I get paid a lot of money doing it, and it is helping me raise my family."

Others find their career through a series of trial and error: "I interned at a dentist's office, and after a day I knew it was not for me." And others end up choosing a career someone else wants for them.

There was a student at my university who was a phenomenal jazz pianist. His professors said he was one of the best they ever had. He told me how much he loved music, but that when he

How did you end up in your current roles in life, in career, in relationship?

returned to South Korea after college he would go into his father's business. "Do you want to be in business?" I asked. He said no, but he had no choice—his father had raised him and paid for him to go to college for the business. His father, not a personal sense of calling, determined his profession.

Many people in our world today do not have the luxury of choosing a vocation. Millions of people wake up each day and engage in work simply to put a roof over their head and food on their table. And there are millions of other people who do have some say over their vocational choices, but see their job as a means to an end—to make money in order to buy things. What is missing in both cases is a sense that our work matters to God, that what we do with our hands and minds in our jobs has anything to do with giving glory to God. There is little sense that we have been *called* in life.

I believe we are all called. We are all called forth by God, and we are all called to do something that God has for our lives. We are all born with a calling—and not just one calling, but many. Our first calling is to be a child—to be daughters and sons of someone. Many people are also called to be siblings. These are our first callings. Then we are called to be students. As adults we may be called into either marriage or singleness. And for some of us, we are called to be parents. At a certain point we may be called to be caretakers of aging parents. And finally, we may be called to be grandparents, and even great-grandparents.

These are all callings, roles we are designed to play. I did not ask to be a male or the youngest in my family. I came into the world this way. I chose to be married, and feel called to the married life, and I love it. I am grateful to be called to be a father—it is one of my favorite callings. I did not enjoy having to take care of aging parents, not because it was a burden but because I hated seeing them suffer. And I look forward to being a grandfather one day, should that happen.

All of these roles are deeply woven into our souls. Our souls are built for these callings. We are all called, called to many things, and each of them matters a great deal to God.

> What are some of the roles you have been called to throughout your life?

TRUE NARRATIVE: YOU ARE CALLED— LARGE *C* AND SMALL *C*

While we are all called to many things, our first and primary calling is to be in relationship with the Trinity. We are all called to be *in Christ*. My friend Dr. Jeff Bjorck, who has taught on the subject of calling for many years, describes this as our "calling with a capital *C*." He distinguishes between this "capital *C* calling" and others, such as vocational callings, which are "small *c* callings." Jeff pointed out to me that the apostle Paul is an excellent example of this. In his greeting to the church at Rome, Paul writes:

> Paul, a servant of Jesus Christ, *called* to be an apostle, set apart for the gospel of God. (Romans 1:1, italics added)

> To all God's beloved in Rome, who are *called* to be saints. (Romans 1:7, italics added)

Paul's "small *c* calling" was to be an apostle, a calling he accepted and fulfilled, even to his death. But he turns to his audience and reminds them that they are "God's beloved . . . called to be saints." This is the capital *C* calling, to be in Christ—indeed, Paul also tells them they are "*called* to belong to Jesus Christ" (Romans 1:6, italics added). Their capital *C* calling is an invitation to loving relationship with God.

The Christ-form of our souls has been designed to be inhabited by the risen Christ. I am grateful to have discovered that my primary call is to be "Jim in whom Christ dwells and delights." As a result of this call, I am also called to be a part of the body of Christ, a member of Jesus' church. This is the primary calling for all of us: to be God's beloved saints who belong to God and are members of Christ's body. From that Calling, all other callings, including vocational callings, can emerge.

VOCATIONAL CALLINGS

When talking about calling, most people start with vocational calling. "What am I going to do with my life?" is the constant question I hear many of my college students asking and often fretting about. When we start with the small *c* calling, we feel enormous pressure to find the bull's-eye, as mentioned above—the one true thing we are called to do.

I find it more helpful to begin with the large *C* calling—to be in Christ, and thus in service to God. The question is not then, "What am I to do that will [e.g., make money, give me prestige, satisfy my parents' desires, make me the most happy]?" The question is rather, "What can I do that will show my love for God and give the most glory to God?"

Each of us is unique. We are each never-to-be-repeated stories of grace, born with innate passions and proclivities. We are born with specific temperaments and talents. We have unique stories—born into different places and cultures and families, and our own individual experiences that no one else has had. These built-in dispositions and abilities, along with our distinctive stories, combine in such a way that we find ourselves suited for several different vocations. And though not true of everyone, many of us have a choice in what we will do with our lives.

Our souls contain a unique dignity, an unrepeatable quality, which is suited for various vocations. We do not know what those are at birth. We do not emerge from the womb with a sign that reads "future lawyer." Our calling, or callings, will gradually manifest themselves over our lifetime. But this presumes that we listen to our life, and listen to the One who calls us. Vocation, after all, comes from the Latin word *vocare*, which means "to be called."

This calling will emerge in subtle and sometimes obvious ways. It will come through the voice of others, through open and closed doors, and through opportunities lost and found. It will come primarily in the form of passion—in a deep longing for something that we cannot escape. And it happens when we view ourselves not as a set of skills to be maximized but as a soul that is to be uplifted.

THE GOODNESS OF WORK

Saint Catherine of Siena said, "Be who God meant you to be and you will set the world on fire." How do we discover the person God means for us to be? To be sure, God has always meant for us to be the things written about in this book: we are wanted by God, we are loved by God, and we are forgiven, made alive, and made holy by God. These are also a part of your calling. When we know these things deep in our souls we will, indeed, set the world on fire. The world is hungry for genuinely transformed people. Also you have a unique story and a deep longing for God, and these are part of your calling: to own your story, and to be in intimate communion with the Trinity.

You are also called to work. A part of the divine calling is the call to have dominion over things: "Then God said, 'Let us make humankind in our image, according to our likeness; and let them have dominion over the fish of the sea, and over the birds of the air, and over the cattle, and over all the wild animals of the earth, and over every creeping thing that creeps upon the earth'" (Genesis 1:26). Humans are called to have say over things. This is tied to our vocations, our callings. Some are called to have dominion over musical notes (e.g., a jazz musician); others are called to have dominion over mathematic equations (e.g., a math professor); still others are called to have dominion over words and ideas (e.g., a journalist).

> Do you view work as "good"? Ask God to give you his view of work.

A *vocation* is an occupation, trade, or profession that a person is called to do and, ideally, for which they are well suited. I have family and friends in law enforcement, medicine, education, insurance, business, sales, publishing, and the law, just to name a few. I have friends who are writers and musicians and artists. A vocation is different from a job.

A job is what we do in order to be paid. In my life, I have had many jobs. I worked in a butcher shop, a lumberyard, and an athletic shoe store while in high school. I mowed lawns and painted houses one summer. I was never called to these jobs; I did them with one aim in mind—to make money.

A vocation, a calling, assumes that one is called to a specific work. For a Christian, the One who calls us is God, and the work he calls us to is good. But hearing the voice of God, and even hearing the voice of our own hearts and our own life, is difficult. It requires discernment, which is an art, not a science. There is no foolproof test to determine our vocation. The aptitude test I took in high school said I should be a forest ranger or a florist. I have no idea how that happened —neither of these professions has any interest for me. But learning to hear, to discern, our calling is not impossible. There are many clues and many sources that can help us find our way into work that is meaningful and fulfilling.

DISCERNING OUR CALLING

A most helpful clue to discerning our calling comes from one of my favorite writers, Frederick Buechner. I was privileged to spend an evening with him when I was in graduate school, and I asked him a lot of questions about discerning vocation. He said, "The best advice I can give you is this: listen to your life. Pay attention to your life. You will find the answer if you listen." I have never forgotten these words, and I have found them to be true.

In one of his books, Buechner says this about discovering our vocation:

> By and large a good rule for finding out is this: the kind of work
> God usually calls you to is the kind of work (a) that you need
> most to do and (b) that the world most needs to have done. . . .
> The place God calls you to is the place where your deep glad-
> ness and the world's deep hunger meet.

I have found this intersection between our own "deep gladness" and
the world's "deep hunger" to be especially useful. But it should not
be treated as a Venn diagram, it is not that simple. There are many
things that make my heart glad, and the world is starving for a lot
of things. Finding the intersection will take more work than an
aptitude test or a diagram. What I love about Buechner's approach
to discernment is where it begins, with what makes us uniquely
who we are.

For many years I was actually afraid to give my life and my will
completely to God. I assumed if I did, I would end up dying as a
martyr on the mission field, which I thought would give God the
greatest glory. If not martyrdom, I assumed God would call me to
something dreadful, because I as-
sumed he was most pleased when
we suffer for God's sake. I have
come to believe those narratives
are not only false, but deadly. God
takes no pleasure in our suffering.
And God created us with desires,

Reflect on some of
your God-given desires.
Are they guiding you
into something new?

and did so for a reason—that they might guide us. Again, there is no
bull's-eye that we either hit or miss. E. J., in the opening story, found
gladness in both business *and* in pastoral ministry, and both jobs
gave glory to God.

FINDING DESTINY IN OUR HANDS AND HEARTS

The great theologian Ray Anderson tells the story of discovering his
callings, and I have found his insights very helpful. When he was a
young man, he grew up on his father's farm. One day Ray took lunch

to his father, who was out working in the field. During lunch his father said, "Son, put your hand in the soil. This soil is your life. Take care of it and it will take care of you." At that time in his life, Ray was very attached to the farm, to the soil, and assumed it was his calling to be a farmer.

After he returned from serving in World War II, he went back to the farm to enter into the same relationship his father had with the soil. His father was pleased, and said, "Now you have found your place, son." Not long after, his father passed away. And not long after that, Ray's emerging life of faith in Jesus began to take central place in his life. As he put it, he felt "dissonance" with his calling to be a farmer. He felt an urge to go to seminary and this calling produced a lot of tension, so he took that step in faith. Six months into his time in seminary, he said, that tension left. He still loved his father and loved the soil, but he felt fully freed to make ministry his next calling.

Looking back, Ray said,

My father had not attached my hand to the soil of a farm— although that is how I had understood it. Rather, he had attempted to attach my hand to my heart. No matter what "soil" my hand was plunged into, if the task was undertaken with my heart, there was a sense of completeness that brought joy and fulfillment.

What a beautiful understanding of calling: no matter which "soil" we plunge our hand into, if we do it with our full heart we find joy and fulfillment.

Ray went on to be ordained, and would serve in the local church for the rest of his life in different capacities. But later he felt called to be a teacher. Ray asked himself another question I found important: "What will satisfy my soul?" This question, he said, helped him discover his *destiny*. His primary call was to be a seminary professor *and* to be a pastor.

How do you find your destiny? Ray Anderson believed the key question is this: "If _____ [fill in the vocation] is the last thing I will ever do on earth, will it be meaningful to me?" For Ray, that was being a teacher, a seminary professor. He said it was his hope to be teaching until the day he died. He was once a farmer and loved it. He was a local church pastor and loved it. But he eventually found his deepest gladness in being a teacher. And I am one of the many people who is glad he did. I was blessed to take a course from Dr. Anderson, and that one course shaped my understanding of ministry more than any other course I took.

Fill in the blank: "If [this vocation] is the last thing I will ever do on earth, will it be meaningful to me?"

Completeness, joy, and fulfillment are wonderful indicators of our calling, because that which makes us sense these things is located deep in our souls. I think this is what Frederick Buechner meant by "deep gladness." I do not mean by gladness that we will find happiness in every aspect of our job. Every vocation has challenges, ups and downs, and aspects we will find difficult. For me, I am grateful to have found my calling and destiny in being a college professor, a writer, and a teaching pastor. All three callings come with their own challenges, but they are all things I love doing, and would do even if I were not paid to do them. Like Ray, I hope to be doing them until I pass over into glory.

FINDING CALLING IN YOUR STORY

I have also come to believe that our callings are intimately connected to our sacred stories. One of my former students, Jimmy, sensed a call to ministry and everyone who knew him affirmed it. He tried working with youth because, he said, he did not feel worthy to minister to adults. He later worked in a dying, inner-city church, laboring to raise it to new life, to no avail. He found the spark that ignited his true calling when he became a military chaplain. This calling made perfect sense in connection to Jimmy's sacred story. Both his father and grandfather had been in the Air Force, so he knew and respected the military from a young age. But both his father and grandfather had gone down wrong paths in life. They suffered from substance abuse, and were abusive to their families. Jimmy once told me that the pain inflicted on his whole family by these two men was devastating.

For Jimmy, becoming a chaplain in the Air Force Chaplain Corps fit him in a way no other ministry work had before. "I saw the great need that existed in the military. I have a deep desire to help military members *not* go down the same path my dad and grandpa did. In a way, I am trying to honor them by helping others." Jimmy has risen in rank and is flourishing in this role. His story is a good example of how we discern our callings. We are all called to something; it is imprinted on our souls and discovered in our stories.

My sister, Vicki, is ten years older than I am. When she was young, my dad changed jobs several times and she had to change schools along with it. This was very hard on her. She would make friends, then have to leave and make new friends all over again. As a result, she was often an outsider. She became very outgoing and also very compassionate toward those who did not fit in; it was a part of why she wanted to be a teacher. But a deeply fulfilling calling came later in life when she began working for the Child Abuse Prevention Agency. Though she was not abused herself, she has a deep compassion for children who are. She works tirelessly, speaking to kids in schools and teaching parenting classes.

It is common for our callings to be related to our own pain or our own positive experiences. Many therapists become therapists because of how much they were healed in their own therapy; many teachers teach because they had at least one teacher who changed their lives. Just as our callings are embedded in our souls, they are also interwoven in our stories. If you are still searching for your calling, one great piece of advice is to listen to your life. And one great question worth asking yourself is this: What would you do if you weren't afraid?

In looking at my own life and at the lives of those I know and love, I have come to the conclusion that we discern our callings best when we are most in tune with God. When the transcendent connection with God is at its strongest, our sense of calling is at its clearest.

> Take time to reflect on your life. What is it saying about your calling? And what would you do if you weren't afraid?

In the quietness, in the stillness, when I am most in tune with God, I have a greater sense of clarity about what I am to be doing in my life. There are many voices clamoring for attention, but only one voice I find reliable when it comes to making decisions about what to do with my life.

CALLINGS IN DIFFERENT SEASONS

Reflecting on the story of E. J., I wonder, as he did, what would have happened if he had gone into local church ministry in his late twenties as opposed to his late fifties. This I do know: E. J. was great at being a pastor in a local church for those eight years. I know this because E. J. is my father-in-law. I witnessed firsthand how much he loved it and how much the people loved him. I saw the church begin to grow and thrive during his tenure. And I watched him step down with grace and gratitude when he retired.

I think there is a seasonal dimension to our calling. There are professions, such as athletics and ballet, which one ages *out* of. But most professions, the ones that are not dependent on physical prowess, are vocations we age *into*.

I love the fruit trees in my backyard. I love to watch them blossom in spring, produce fruit in summer, gloriously fade into autumn, and remain dormant in the winter—still very much alive but

> Have you begun a new season of your callings in your life? Or do you sense a new season of calling?

resting. In our lives there are times of great growth, and times of quiet rebuilding. I am not the same teacher I was thirty years ago when I started. I miss some of the exuberance, but I don't miss the naiveté; I miss the innocence, but I treasure the wisdom.

In every season our soul is awake and speaking to us. It longs to be desired, to be loved, to be forgiven, to be alive, to be holy, to own its story, to connect to God, and to engage in meaningful work. The good and beautiful you longs for a good and beautiful life of purpose and joy. God has designed you for all of this, and God, in Christ and through the Spirit, makes this a reality. By grace you have been made, by grace you have been saved, and by grace you will one day be glorified and rule and reign in the heavens for all eternity.

Listen to the verbs

"The Unfurling"
Let us celebrate the gradual opening
Of a banner taking its place in the world;
A long unraveling and a fine unwinding,
Like a flower unwrapping itself from itself,
A parcel of thinking softly untying
Or an origami of ideas hugely unfolding
As, caught by the breeze, image and language
Spread their twin messages into the air.
IAN MCMILLAN

"Within you is a fathomless reservoir of possibilities and your soul's capacity is deeper than any ocean." Though there are many ways to live out our various callings, including vocational calling, we can get some hints about the *qualities* of our calling in a fun exercise where we notice what verbs, what action words, make our heart soar and bring us joy. As Julia Cameron says, "What we really want to do is what we are really meant to do."

As you scan your life and listen to it a moment, you will not need to conjure up words or pick them out of thin air. Notice *you* going about daily life, experiences, travels, conversations, work, play, and rest. Even if you aren't in the specific job that would be most suited to your design, your design is and has been showing itself in all aspects of your life, because God has made you to be who you are.

In this exercise, look for the activities/actions that express your unique "this-ness." It's not that each action itself is unique to you, but the combination of these actions and your "you-ness" in the action is what is unique.

1. Notice fifteen activities/actions that fill you with joy or deep satisfaction. Write them in the form of a gerund, which is a verb plus "ing." So if you like to negotiate, write "negotiating."

2. From your list of fifteen, choose your favorite seven. I know—it's hard.

3. From your list of seven, choose your favorite four. I know—it's even harder.

4. Now craft sentences or phrases (it can be just one phrase if they all fit together) that describe how you see yourself living out these verbs.

Here's an example someone did, but the form isn't as important as just noticing and capturing in words what you love. The seven words chosen from the fifteen verbs are starred. The four chosen from the seven are double-starred.

- dancing **
- sparkling *
- teaching
- mentoring
- receiving *
- designing **
- plunging
- discovering
- adventuring **
- imagining

- overflowing **
- solving
- connecting
- achieving
- experiencing *

  These are the crafted phrases putting those actions together:

- being filled to overflowing
- dancing (perichoresis) within the Trinity
- designing experiences and adventures that invite others into the dance

This person seems called to a type of ministry, but do not think that you need to be. Your crafted phrases could be about engineering or artistry or scuba-diving. Be you.

> God's creative call is revealed in my deepest self. In some way this call is my deepest self. It is not a call that I have but a call that I am. An Infinite Love tenderly called me forth out of nowhere and nothingness; an unspeakable Love emptied itself to redeem the identity that I lost sight of in sinfulness; an enlightening Love keeps calling me back to what I am.

eleven

YOU WILL BE GLORIFIED

On September 19, 1997, Christian singer, songwriter, and recording artist Rich Mullins died in a car crash. He was one of my closest friends. He had lived with our family, in our attic apartment, for two years, and we spent many late nights talking about faith and life and the Bible and the church. I was in Dallas, Texas, to officiate a wedding at the time of his death. I was informed he had died an hour before the actual wedding. I was stunned and in shock, but I held it together for the sake of the couple during the service.

At the wedding reception I could not hold it together any longer. I went out to a field and fell to my knees, crying, in the middle of a thunderstorm. The rain mixed with my tears as I cried out to the sky, "Are you okay? Are you okay?" More than anything else, I just wanted to know that my friend was okay. It was not my loss that I cared about in that moment, it was his well-being. Then I heard a voice. It was Rich's voice, whispering in the wind, saying, "I'm okay. Don't worry about me. I am more than okay." Those words I heard in the storm carried me through my grief for many years: "I am okay. . . . I am more than okay."

The pain of parting is real, but the failure to believe in continued life beyond death is the source of our fear about death. If we believed —really believed—that our loved ones who have passed are "more than okay," if we were certain—really certain—that their life has continued in a meaningful way, the fear of death would lose its sting.

> Do you believe you are an "unceasing spiritual being with an eternal destiny in God's great universe"?

This reality is something we hope for, not only for our loved ones, but also for ourselves. The fear of dying haunts all of us, all of the time, though perhaps not in a palpable way until we get older and people we know and love die. The resurrection of Jesus is the ground of our hope for life everlasting. But it will take a leap with faith to believe that we are *unceasing spiritual beings with an eternal destiny in God's great universe*. It is challenging for us to believe this, but it is what Jesus has promised.

FALSE NARRATIVE: WHEN WE DIE, WE ARE GONE FOREVER

Similar to the "accidental little lumps of something" (the false narrative discussed in chapter three) is the narrative that "when we die, we are gone forever." This narrative teaches that we are only a memory when we are no more, and that the same is true for all of our loved ones. This is one of the deepest fears humans have and have had for all time. Nonexistence is unconscionable; we simply cannot conceive of it.

This narrative exists because no one, except Jesus, has died and returned to tell us about an afterlife with any real credibility. There are certainly a lot of people who have had a near death experience (NDE), who have "died" for a time (a minute or two or more) and come back to life with stories to tell about what they saw. There are many such experiences, and they witness to something about life after death, though there is not a lot of consistency. Though stories about NDEs offer a kind of hope, New Testament scholar Scot McKnight cautions us not to put too much stock in them. Perhaps NDE stories offer a peek into the afterlife, McKnight acknowledges, but he says, "I don't believe in Heaven on the basis that people have been there and come back. I believe in Heaven because God promised it."

Still, the idea of dying creates dissonance in our embodied souls. Perhaps this is because our souls know that we were not made to die. Perhaps that dissonance we feel about death comes from the fact that we actually are unceasing spiritual beings, people who will not be gone when we die, but will be glorified.

TRUE NARRATIVE: WHEN WE DIE, WE WILL BE GLORIFIED FOREVER

The teaching of the New Testament offers a very different view of death. In writing to the Thessalonian Christians, in what is thought to be one of the earliest epistles, Paul encourages them in their concern about Christians who have died. Many of them believed Jesus would return soon—so what happens to those who died before the second coming? Are they "okay," so to speak? Paul says this to them:

> But we do not want you to be uninformed, brothers and sisters, about those who have died, so that you may not grieve as others do who have no hope. For since we believe that Jesus died and rose again, even so, through Jesus, God will bring with him those who have died. (1 Thessalonians 4:13-14)

Paul affirms the fact that they are grieving, but does not want them to grieve as others do. He wants them to *grieve with hope* because of one important truth: Jesus died and rose again. Jesus' resurrection, in addition to imparting new life, as discussed in this book, is also the foundation of the hope of our resurrection after death.

Paul knows that grief is real. And he knows that it is easy for us to lose heart when those we love die. This is why he tells the Corinthian

Christ-followers that even though our bodies age and die, we are being prepared for "an eternal weight of glory":

> So we do not lose heart. Even though our outer nature is wasting away, our inner nature is being renewed day by day. For this slight momentary affliction is preparing us for an eternal weight of glory beyond all measure, because we look not at what can be seen but at what cannot be seen; for what can be seen is temporary, but what cannot be seen is eternal. (2 Corinthians 4:16-18)

Outwardly we waste away—we see the wrinkles in the mirror—but there is a deeper reality, a spiritual renewal that is happening each day. The life we are living now is preparing us for something greater than we can imagine. That is why Paul says we must look not at what can be seen, which is temporary, but at what cannot be seen, which is the eternal kind of life that is in us when we are born from above.

List some ways you can focus on the unseen, on eternal realities, every day.

This kind of life is in us and is also "hidden in Christ." Paul tells the Christ-followers in Colossae to have hope, because "you have died, and your life is hidden with Christ in God. When Christ who is your life is revealed, then you also will be revealed with him in glory" (Colossians 3:3-4). We have *already* died, died to the life we had before Jesus. And we rose with him—we have been made alive together with Christ. And that life is now safely hidden in Christ. When Christ, who is our true life, is revealed—when Jesus returns to establish the new heaven and new earth—*we will be revealed with him in glory*. Put simply, we are going to glow. That is our destiny. Our hope of heaven is built on what Jesus has done.

Jesus abolished death. He simply did away with it. What the false narrative assumes—that we die and no longer exist—will never actually happen to those who have entered into Jesus' eternal kind of life, as he promised. This is because those who are loved by God will not be allowed to cease to be. God will not have this. Those who live in fellowship with God are his treasures. What else would God do with his treasure? Let it no longer be? God delights in us, and intends to keep us forever.

Jesus said he was preparing places for his human sisters and brothers to one day join him. On the day he was crucified, he told the thief on the cross next to him that he would be with him that very day in a place Jesus called "paradise." Jesus even said, "Very truly, I tell you, whoever keeps my word will never see death" (John 8:51). It is crucial that we see that none of this is dependent on what we do to merit or accomplish this. Just as we did nothing to enter life, we do nothing to destroy death—it is all the work of God, in Christ. In the song "Smitten, Pt. 2" by the group Penny and Sparrow, Death comes upon the manger and, foreseeing the emptying tomb, says to Jesus, "When You're old enough to speak, You will undo me." Death has been undone by the One who came in a manger and rose from a tomb.

Jesus was casual about death. He brought people from death to life in several places in the Gospels. This is a foreshadowing of the general resurrection. Each healing—when the blind could see and the lame could walk—was a sign that God, in Jesus, had power over the natural world as we know it. Jesus could be dismissive about death because he knew the power of eternal life. All of the miracles were signs that point to something else. Jesus could turn water into wine and a sack lunch into a banquet for the masses. The hope of heaven is built on the work of Jesus then, and now, and in the life to come.

THE RELIABILITY OF HEAVEN

How can we know that heaven is the destiny of those loved ones who have died, and our destiny as well? If NDEs are not reliable sources in which to place our confidence, what is? Scot McKnight, in his marvelous book *The Heaven Promise*, offers five elements that establish the reliability of the promise of heaven. They are:

- God is making the promise.
- God's promise is heaven.
- God makes this promise to us and for us.
- God has entered into a covenant with us to make the Heaven Promise good, a binding covenant on which he stakes his life and integrity.
- We are asked to trust God's promise.

It is not the *amount* of our faith but the *object* of our faith that matters. The object of our faith is God. God is the one making the promise.

And the promise is about heaven. God is saying to us, in Jesus and through the Spirit, that we are destined to rule and reign with God in glory. The emphasis is on God, not us. We are not the ones establishing this reality. It is not created by us, or dependent on us. It is not based on our promises—thanks be to God, because our promises are unreliable. It all comes down to *trust*. We trust in someone when we have experienced their reliability. The God who has not failed us in the past, the God who is faithful to us in the present, is the same God who will not fail us in the future—on this we can rely.

> Can you personally rely on God's promises?
> Think about some specific times he did not fail you in the past.

In contrast to the dissonance we feel in our embodied souls at the thought of death, I have found a great deal of *consonance* in the promise that those I love are safe, and that I also will not die but will be glorified. This sits very well in my soul. When I think about being reunited with those I have lost, my heart is strangely warmed, and my soul is glad.

THE SOUL IS NOT AFRAID

John O'Donohue was a Celtic Christian author whose writings have always moved me. This is no more true than his writing on the nature of the soul in light of death. He makes the point that while our mind cannot process death, our soul is understanding and hopeful and unafraid. He writes,

> While the knowing of the mind is limited by frontiers, the soul has no frontiers. At death, the mind is up against the last and ultimate frontier. It will attempt to understand and, with dignity and hope, accept what is ending and what is coming. However, the soul knows in a different way. The soul is not afraid. It has no reason to be afraid, for death cannot touch the soul.

Death cannot touch the soul, because the soul has no frontiers, no border it cannot cross. The mind cannot comprehend the wilderness of life after death, a place we have never been. But it is not too much for the soul. Our souls easily pass over borders.

Our soul knows that death is not the end but the beginning, not a departure but a homecoming. O'Donohue writes,

> For your soul, death is a homecoming. Naturally the soul will feel the sadness of withdrawal from the visible world. Ultimately, however, physical death must also be an adventure for the soul. There must be excitement for the soul at the edge of such transformation, and joy in bringing the bright essence of a life's harvest into eternity.

He is saying that, instead of something to be feared, physical death is "an adventure for the soul," filled with excitement and joy. What a sharp contrast to how we often think about death. True, we will feel sadness as we withdraw from this world and all of its wonder, but something greater awaits us. And our souls know it.

THE WEIGHT OF GLORY

All of us live with what C. S. Lewis called "an inconsolable secret," a hidden longing for glory: "Glory means good report with God, acceptance by God, response, acknowledgment and welcome into the heart of things." This longing will be met, he says, when the "door on which we have been knocking all our lives will open at last." Every time we enter a room longing to be welcomed, or hear about a party to which we hope to be invited, we are touching this inconsolable secret. I love surprise birthday parties for this reason. When the birthday boy or girl suddenly realizes a whole party has been planned for them, and that people have done so because of how much they love them, there is a look of joy on their faces I have found unmatched.

This is what it means to be glorified. When Paul tells the Colossians that when Christ is revealed they will also be revealed in glory, he has in mind this sort of welcome—a birthday party on steroids, a grand celebration of who we truly are in the eyes of God. I like to think about this, not so much for me, but for those I love. Lewis points out that it is good for us to think about the future glorification of others:

> It may be possible for each to think too much of his own potential glory hereafter; it is hardly possible for him to think too often or too deeply about that of his neighbor. The load, or weight, or burden of my neighbor's glory should be laid daily on my back, a load so heavy that only humility can carry it, and the backs of the proud will be broken.

The weight of glory that awaits our brothers and sisters in Christ is something we do well to ponder. When I think about the future glory of my wife and children and family members, of the women and men who have been so important to me, I am moved to doxology. And to a deep sense of humility, as Lewis notes, which is required if I am to see them rightly.

Every time we see suffering there is dissonance in our souls. Every news feed that tells a story about violence and abuse and death makes our souls recoil.

> Take some time to ponder the potential glory of your brothers and sisters in Christ.

Our souls know that this is not the way it is supposed to be. The pain of the pandemic caused by Covid-19 will last for a generation. It is something we cannot unsee or unfeel. The dissonance is unbearable, but the hope of a time and a place when sorrow is ended causes a consonance in our embodied souls that cannot be denied.

GLORIFYING GRACE

Throughout this book I have been writing about the *grace* of God in every chapter. Grace is God's action in our lives—a gift we do not merit or deserve or earn, but that is freely given to us by God. Grace imparts to us what we could never achieve on our own. So far I have been writing about the three classic theological works of grace: prevenient grace, justifying grace, and sanctifying grace. We come into this world with a "spark" of grace on our souls—a transcendent longing for God, and a soul that longs to be desired and loved. That is *prevenient* grace—it comes previous to our birth, a gift we are born with. But we are born under the power and penalty of sin, so we need more grace! *Justifying* grace (sometimes called *justification*) breaks the penalty of sin by Jesus' work on the cross—Jesus frees us from the penalty of sin. But that is not all there is to saving grace. Jesus' resurrection imparts new life, or regeneration, in believers. This is *sanctifying* grace, whereby the power of sin has been broken.

There is a fourth work of grace—namely, *glorification*, which is the focus of this chapter. Glorification refers to the final state of believers upon Jesus' return. Our bodies will be physically resurrected, and we will receive a resurrection body—a body just like Jesus' resurrection body. Jesus' body after resurrection was both physical and spiritual. Mysteriously, Jesus could eat fish on the beach with his disciples and also walk through a wall. Our bodies will be bodies—we will not be ghosts. And we will be recognizable to those who knew us on this earth, though not perhaps immediately, as in what happened to the disciples on the road to Emmaus. They only recognized Jesus in the breaking of bread.

While justification frees us from the *penalty* of sin, and sanctification frees us from the *power* of sin, glorification frees us from the *presence* of sin. In the new creation—the new heaven and new earth—there is no more sin. That is why there will be no more suffering and sorrow, which are byproducts of sin. So what will we be doing—will we have any fun if there is no "sin"? In the new creation we will be engaged in all kinds of work, we will be endlessly creative. We will not be wearing angel's wings and playing harps while sitting on clouds, as depicted in medieval artwork. We will not be standing forever in a worship service that never has a benediction.

> Justification frees us from the *penalty* of sin, sanctification frees us from the *power* of sin, and glorification frees us from the *presence* of sin.

Rather, we will merge with everything that is beautiful and good, and we will discover then what we only glimpse occasionally now: that all of life can be an act of worship, and that the absence of sin brings true joy and completely transforms the very nature of life and work. We need to have a robust view of heaven in order to live with the anticipation it deserves. God designed you and me with incredible capacities to dream, imagine, and create. Without the pull of sin, imagine what we can do! God would love nothing more than to assign each of us something magnificent to do—perhaps you will be assigned to run a galaxy.

WHAT WILL HEAVEN BE LIKE?

What will heaven be like? This is a question for which we long to find an answer. According to cartoons, there will be clouds and harps and streets of gold. According to jokes, there will be Saint Peter at the check-in, with some cheeky wisecrack about who gets in and who doesn't. For many it is a place of unending pleasure—a nonstop, all-access pass to an amusement park. For others it is a nonstop church service, where God is praised endlessly by a chorus of humans and angels. The problem is this: we simply do not have much information when it comes to specifics about what heaven will be like.

The Bible's references to heaven are few, and mostly metaphorical. Take for example "streets of gold" (Revelation 21:21). Should we take this literally? I am not sure if streets made of gold are even a good idea—I think there would be traction issues. The biblical images are attempts to show the precious nature of the next world. Gold is precious in this life, so why not imagine streets covered in it? The problem with all metaphors and similes is that they break down.

I wrote a book called *Room of Marvels*, a fictional work about a man who suffers a lot of loss and is given a dream in which he goes to heaven. It is a work of fiction, and I make no claim that I have some secret insight into what heaven will be like. I wrote the book as a part of my own healing. The idea that the things that happen in this life matter, that they prepare us for an eternal weight of glory; the notion that those I love are well; the idea that one day there will be no more sorrow, is very healing—it was for me.

I was on a few radio talk shows after the book came out, and in a few of them the host allowed callers to ask me questions. I was surprised by a few things from this experience. One, the deep hunger for heaven is very real. We all need to know that there is a happy ending. And two, I was stunned at how many people asked me if their pets would be in heaven. But then I thought, *Of course they want to know!*—the things we love in this life are precious, and we don't want to lose them. I don't have an answer, but I defer again to my friend and Bible scholar Scot McKnight, whose answer to the question is yes—there will be pets in heaven.

Again, the problem is that we do not know. We can surmise that all that is good and beautiful and true will be in heaven. And we can know that God, in Christ, has done all God can to make sure people have access to heaven. Beyond that we can only speculate. People have asked me a stunning variety of questions about heaven: "If a child dies on earth, what age will they be in heaven?" "Will we be married in heaven?" "Will we remember our life on earth?" The list goes on and on. The best answer I can give to the question, "What will heaven be like?" is one I once heard Dallas Willard give when he was asked: "Well, I don't know for sure, but I do know what God is like and that God is good, so whatever it is like I am certain we will all say, 'This is a great idea!'"

> What do you think heaven will be like? Do you believe it will be good because God is good?

GRIEVING WITH HOPE

On May 8, 2013, my mentor and friend Dallas Willard graduated to glory. I had a trip planned to see him, but he died before I could get there. There was a private funeral planned, and later, a memorial service. I wanted to be at the funeral—Dallas was like a father to me, a spiritual father. His death wrecked me. Jane (his wife) and Becky (his daughter) asked if I would be a pallbearer, and I said yes. It would be an honor to help carry to his resting place the man who had carried my soul for years. I sat next to my friend John Ortberg at the funeral, who was also a pallbearer. Of all the funerals I have ever attended, this one was the most peaceful, because if there was anyone you were certain had crossed over into the heavens upon death, it was Dallas.

At the graveside service, the small group of us were given a rose and asked to place it on the coffin. One by one we did. As I approached the coffin I took two petals from the rose to keep and placed them in my pocket. I wanted something to remember him by. After the funeral had ended, Jane invited me to their home. When we were there she said, "Have you seen the list of people Dallas titled, 'Our Boys Who Are Out There'?" I said no. She took me to his office, and above his desk was a handwritten piece of paper with a list of names on it, and she pointed out my name. "Dallas was very proud of you, and he prayed for you and the others on this list, that you would continue the good work of advancing the kingdom of God." I started to cry. Jane made a copy of the list and let me keep it.

After I left their home, I did not know what to do. So I drove down to Malibu, and went and sat on a pier, holding my petals, the list, and the bulletin for the funeral. I noticed a quote from Dietrich Bonhoeffer on the back of the bulletin. It read:

> There is nothing that can replace the absence of someone dear to us, and one should not even attempt to do so. One must simply hold out and endure it. At first that sounds very hard, but at the same time it is also a great comfort. For to the extent the emptiness truly remains unfilled one remains connected to the other person through it. It is wrong to say that God fills the emptiness. God in no way fills it but much more leaves it precisely unfilled and thus helps us preserve—even in pain—the authentic relationship. Furthermore, the more beautiful and full the remembrances, the more difficult the separation. But gratitude transforms the torment of memory into silent joy. One bears what was lovely in the past not as a thorn but as a precious gift deep within, a hidden treasure of which one can always be certain.

I read this quote over and over. Bonhoeffer was right: we want to be rid of the pain of the absence and emptiness we feel when someone we love passes, but we must not ask for that. It is our connection with them. It preserves the "authentic relationship." And he was also right that the more beautiful the remembrances, the more difficult the separation. John Pavlovitz has said that grief is the tax on loving people. If this is true, that explains why the more we love, the more profound the grief. Pavlovitz concludes, "Grief is a small penalty for the immeasurable treasure of loving and being loved."

I sat in the California sunshine, misty eyed, as I recalled all of my most precious memories of time spent with Dallas. His deep baritone voice singing hymns, the way he choked up when he preached because he was so moved by God's love, the dry humor, the deep wisdom, and the way he gently listened with compassion. I remembered how Dallas comforted me in the death of my daughter Madeline, as he shared how he and Jane had lost twin boys, who were stillborn. I remembered times we sat in airports waiting for our plane, and how he used the time to pray and read the Bible.

As I remembered with gratitude all of these moments, the last part of Bonhoeffer's quote became even more true: "Gratitude transforms the torment of memory into silent joy." Joy because of God. Dallas was now ruling and reigning in the heavens with the God he knew so well, not because of anything Dallas had done or accomplished, but because the God who created him, loved him, forgave him, and raised him to new life *in this life* had raised him again to new life *in the next.*

> Write this down in your journal and take some time to reflect on it: *hope is certainty in a good future.*

We grieve, as Paul said, as those who have hope. And Dallas taught me the definition of hope: certainty in a good future. Not wishful thinking. Certainty. Dallas, I could imagine, was now with Madeline, and with Rich Mullins, and one day, I would join them as well.

REPRISE: *THE GOOD AND BEAUTIFUL YOU*
When I look at the totality of my life, and the longings of my soul, and the stunningly beautiful way God satisfies those longings, I am

moved to doxology. And when I think of you—the good and beautiful you, who is reading this book—I am humbled and honored that you have taken this journey with me. You are no mere mortal. You are a divinely designed, deeply loved, fully forgiven, fully alive, sacred person, with a sacred story of grace, a sacred body, and a holy longing for God. You were perfectly designed before the foundation of this world, to do great works that give glory to God. And you are an unceasing spiritual being with an eternal destiny in God's great universe. You are one in whom Christ dwells and delights. And you will live forever in the strong and unshakable kingdom of God. May you sing and dance with the joy of a child in the knowledge of God's unending love.

celebration

The opening soul-training exercise in this book is holy leisure—doing nothing, for God's sake. The narrative this practice reinforces is, "You are not in control, you did nothing to be here, God does not need you to run the universe, so be at peace, relax." The closing soul-training exercise for this book is *celebration*. Celebration is the natural concluding exercise of this book because we celebrate all that God has done and will do for us. We celebrate because we know that no matter how much suffering there is in this life, there is far more joy that awaits us in the next.

The central theme of this book is this: you have a soul, it has deep needs, and Jesus fulfills those needs. This book is a celebration of who we are, so it is fitting that we end with the future of what God will do for us and allow that future to enter into our present. We do this through the practice of *celebration*. This is not celebration for the sake of celebration, but a celebration of what Jesus has done for and in and through us.

"Celebration is at the heart of the way of Christ," writes Richard J. Foster. And Dallas Willard liked to say, "God is the most joyous being in the universe," which always shocked people to hear. But the Trinity is not grim. God the Father, Son, and Holy Spirit are alive and filled with joy. Celebration is a way we participate in the life of the Trinity. We are called into a "jubilee of the Spirit."

Celebration, as a discipline for the spiritual life, makes us joyful and strong.

Celebration is something we love to do—there are countless holidays and birthdays and special occasions, such as engagements and baby showers, weddings and retirement parties. While those can all be wonderful, the kind of celebration I am encouraging you to engage in this week is an intentional act of celebrating the goodness of God. Celebration is actually a discipline. And it is something our souls long for. Not the wild parties where people get intoxicated on a substance in order to feel good, but a joyful gathering where people celebrate the goodness of God.

Celebration, writes Adele Calhoun, is "a way of engaging in actions that orient the spirit, the transcendent dimension within us, to worship, praise and thanksgiving," as well as "delighting in all the attentions and never-changing presence of the Trinity." These are needs of the soul. Our souls are made for delight, which is why we seek pleasure so often. But the delight that our soul finds most nourishing is delighting in the Lord. This does not mean that our celebration has to be of a religious nature. We can sing and dance, we can have fun and laugh, and we can feast with our friends, as ways of celebrating. What matters is the object of our celebration. It is not just an excuse to have fun.

We celebrate the God who celebrates us. God, we are told in the Bible, sings over us:

> The Lord, your God, is in your midst,
>   a warrior who gives victory;
> he will rejoice over you with gladness,
>   he will renew you in his love;
> he will exult over you with loud singing
>   as on a day of festival. (Zephaniah 3:17-18)

God rejoiced at your birth, and said it was *very* good. And God rejoices over you every single moment of your life.

The joy that awaits us in the new creation is beyond what we can ever imagine. But the discipline of celebration is a kind of preparation. It is a foretaste of the glory divine. So, how do we engage in the practice of celebration? The following are ways I have found helpful:

- Invite friends over for a "thanksgiving" meal—not the usual Thanksgiving holiday in November, but a gathering to give thanks for great things God has done and is doing.

- Host a dance party. My friends Matt and Catherine host a dance party in their home as a way to allow people to gather and dance and not feel self-conscious. They even have a mirror ball!

- Relish a good comedy movie or stand-up comedy routine—assuming you can find one that fits your taste and sense of decency.

- Make a routine family event special. Every month or two our family gathers for a special brunch in which we prepare everyone's favorite foods.

- Take advantage of existing holidays and festivals: Christmas, Easter, All Saints' Day, May Day, etc. Make them real celebrations of God, and not merely an excuse to throw a party.

We celebrate because our souls love it. We celebrate because God commands it: "Rejoice in the Lord always; again I will say, Rejoice" (Philippians 4:4). We celebrate because our God is the most joyous being in the universe. And we celebrate as a way to remind us that when Christ, who is our life, appears, we will also appear with him in glory.

acknowledgments

People ask me, "How long does it take you to write your books?" and I don't know how to answer, because every book has been different for me. This book was the most difficult book for me to write and it took a long time to write, mostly because *theological anthropology* (the scholarly term for "the nature of the human person") is a challenging subject. Thankfully, I had a lot of help along the way.

I would first like to thank Michael J. Cusick, who I mention in the book as my helpful counselor, therapist, and friend. Michael not only helped me get into the right place for me to write this, but also taught me key concepts and ideas that shaped this book in many ways.

Another person I would like to acknowledge is Fr. Adrian van Kaam. Though he passed over to glory many years ago, and though I never met him, his writings had a deep and profound influence on this book. I am grateful that he labored and studied and wrote so many wonderful volumes on the *science* of formation, and I hope that this book in some way leads people to his work. He is quoted in nearly every chapter, and I could have included many more of his brilliant insights. I am also grateful for Dr. Susan Muto, who worked for many years with Fr. Adrian and wrote many books with him.

Thank you, Susan, for discussing Fr. Van Kaam's work with me and helping me understand his great insights. One other person who helped me understand the writings of Adrian van Kaam is Dr. Rebecca Letterman. Thank you, Rebecca, for our conversations about his work. I recommend the book Susan and Rebecca wrote about the teachings of Fr. Adrian, called *Understanding Our Story*.

And as with most of my books, I am indebted to Dr. Dallas Willard. His theological anthropology, seen most clearly in his brilliant book *Renovation of the Heart*, has shaped my understanding, and thus this book, in too many ways to name.

Thanks to Joe Davis, who first gave me the idea that this book was needed.

And special thanks to Betsy McPeak, who was a graduate student of mine, and who served as a research assistant for me on this book. And more than that, she also collaborated with me on the soul-training exercises and the group discussion guide. Betsy, thank you for your wisdom and encouragement.

I would also like to acknowledge the great help that Chris Kettler, professor of theology and my longtime colleague at Friends University, provided for this book. Chris has read nearly all of my books and offered good theological and biblical feedback to help me avoid pitfalls, and to keep the ideas within the bounds of the great theologians who have gone before us, such as Thomas Torrance, Karl Barth, and Ray Anderson.

I would also like to thank Ben Davis for his careful reading of this book and the helpful feedback he gave me on many occasions.

My longtime friend Dr. Jeff Bjorck played a significant role in helping me navigate the challenging issues in psychology and theology that this book deals with. Jeff, thank you for taking so much time to read it carefully and thoughtfully, and for your excellent ideas and insights.

I would also like to thank Parker Morris, who read this book thoroughly and offered me great perspectives and ideas along the way.

My wife, Meghan, as always, is my supporter and champion, and without her support I could never finish something as daunting as writing a book, especially this one.

I also want to acknowledge my daughter Hope, for supporting me, encouraging me, cheering for me, and for having the courage to let me tell her story.

And I am grateful for my literary agent—but more importantly, "Writer Whisperer"—Kathryn Helmers, for standing with me from start to finish, and at crucial times helping me find my way when it was not clear.

I would also like to thank my editor, and friend, Cindy Bunch, at InterVarsity Press, who patiently walked through this book with me, and was the first person to read it in its entirety and offer great editorial suggestions.

I want to acknowledge the great help I was given by the two focus groups who read through the book, engaged in the soul-training exercises, and used the group guide in order to "field test" it. The first group, led by my sister and brother-in-law, Vicki and Scott Price, was their Apprentice Group in Salina, Kansas. Thank you Salinians!

And the second group of readers, at Chapel Hill UMC in Wichita, Kansas, are Heather and Mike Alumbaugh, Arlene Amis, Margaret Anderson, Dan and Jenny Bennett, Jayne Fry, George Houle, Jan Longhofer, David Nelson, Rene Patton, Andrew Peters, Lynne and Rus Pinkerton, Kelly Sooter, Diana and Jack Storm, Wes Darnell, Alaina Madden, and Deb Kivett. Your input and feedback was invaluable.

Finally, it may seem strange, but I would also like to acknowledge the Trinity—the Father, Son, and Holy Spirit—whose power and presence I felt while studying and writing and editing this book more than with any other book I have written.

Appendix

small Group Discussion Guide

Betsy McPeak and James Bryan smith

CHAPTER 1: YOU HAVE A SOUL

OPENING TO GOD [5 MINUTES]
Begin your group discussion with five minutes of silence. *Why five minutes of silence?* We live in a busy, fast-paced, noisy world where so much is clamoring for our attention. Silence is a gift to let our souls breathe. You rarely know what a person has been through in their day before they arrived at your group. They may be coming from a difficult conversation with their boss or from the stress of a traffic jam. Silence will give grace to transition their presence from where they've been into your group conversation. Silence is also the beginning of listening. This time is set aside to listen to God's voice in the spiritual journey of others, as well as in your own journey as you share this adventure together. Follow your time of silence with an

invitational prayer for God to be with you and to guide your group conversations. May the words of your mouths and the meditations of your hearts be acceptable in God's sight.

SOUL TRAINING [15-20 MINUTES]

If your group is larger than seven people, divide into small groups of three or four. Invite any of those who practiced holy leisure to share how their experience was. After all who want to share have done so, you might consider these questions together:

1. What did you find most difficult in your practice of holy leisure?

2. How did God meet you in holy leisure?

3. What did you learn about yourself and God as you practiced holy leisure?

ENGAGING THE CHAPTER [25-45 MINUTES]

[*Note:* Each week be sure to read through all of the questions before you begin your discussion. You may not have time to get to all of the questions, depending on how many are in your group and how the conversation goes, so be sure to think through which questions you especially want to discuss, to make sure you get to those.]

The main idea of this chapter is that even though it is invisible, and often denied or neglected, the most real thing about us is our soul. Our soul longs, above all else, to be unconditionally loved by God. Our soul cares about all that is most important in life, all that is good and true and beautiful.

1. What has been your understanding of the *soul*? Do you think much about your soul? If so, in what ways? If not, why do you think you seldom think about it?

2. A central point made by the author is that we are *embodied souls*, or *ensouled bodies*, stressing the truth that the soul and the body are united and not separated (which is the mistaken teaching called *dualism*). Why is this important?

3. On pages 13-16 the author says that it is a false narrative that we are a self, and a true narrative that we are a soul. What are the differences between the self and the soul? Do these narratives help you make sense of life?

4. There are ten things listed that our souls cannot endure (p. 18), and ten things that our souls need (pp. 20-21):

Cannot Endure

- Harm to our bodies
- Feeling unwanted
- Guilt
- Shame
- Disconnection from God
- Boredom
- Sin
- Being victimized
- Meaninglessness
- Nonexistence

Soul Needs

- To see my body as sacred
- To be wanted, desired
- To be loved without condition
- To be intimately connected to God
- To be forgiven forever
- To be alive and empowered to adventure
- To be holy, virtuous
- To own my story
- To feel called to a life of purpose
- To be glorified and live forever

Is it a good thing that God made our souls in such a way that they cannot endure those things in the top list? Why or why not? Which one in the "cannot endure" list do you struggle with most? What might be blocking you from receiving the corresponding gift from the "soul needs" list?

5. On page 22 the author says that "the good news is that the God who created our needy souls has, by grace, provided all that our souls will ever need. We cannot achieve or attain these things our souls need. They have to be given to us by God, as a gift. And God has provided all of those things in Jesus." How does that good news seem to you?

6. Are you aware of ways in which you personally try to achieve or attain what your soul needs? What happens as a result of that strain to get your God-given needs met? How would it look to change that dynamic, to live in sync with the good news described?

7. The purpose of this book is stated on page 24: "The rest of this book will examine how God, in Christ, has created the good and beautiful you and has provided for the deepest needs of your soul. Each chapter will examine these actions of God on your behalf and my behalf." What thoughts and feelings does that stir up in you?

ENGAGING SCRIPTURE [10-15 MINUTES]

Have a volunteer read the following Scriptures aloud slowly, and then use the questions below as a discussion guide: Genesis 1:26-27; Jeremiah 1:5; and Ephesians 1:4.

1. Who is the source of your soul? What implications does that have?

2. What does it mean to be made in the image of God?

3. How could we be chosen in Christ before the foundation of the world and consecrated before we were born? Close your eyes and prayerfully consider what this means about you.

GO IN PEACE [5 MINUTES]

Conclude by having everyone close their eyes while one person reads the words below. Other participants hold out cupped hands and imagine receiving the gifts one by one as they are read. The reader then asks, while each gift is still in their hands, "Do you receive this gift?" Participants respond, "Yes, Lord, by your grace I receive this gift." Then they press the gift into their heart as a bodily sign of their intention to receive the gift from God. Participants then hold their cupped hands out again to receive the next gift. (You might want to practice the movements once before actually starting, so everyone knows what to do.)

1. God gave you a soul. (pause) Do you receive this gift?

2. God desires you. (pause) Do you receive this gift?

3. God loves you. (pause) Do you receive this gift?

4. God forgives you. (pause) Do you receive this gift?

5. God gives you life. (pause) Do you receive this gift?

6. God inhabits you with holiness. (pause) Do you receive this gift?

7. God writes your story with you. (pause) Do you receive this gift?

8. God gave you a sacred body. (pause) Do you receive this gift?

9. God is intimately connected to you. (pause) Do you receive this gift?

10. God calls you to a life of purpose. (pause) Do you receive this gift?

11. God glorifies you and gives you life everlasting. (pause) Do you receive this gift?

May your soul go in peace, being filled to overflowing.

NEXT WEEK

In chapter two the theme is that you have a sacred body. The soul-training exercise of moving will train you to live incarnationally.

CHAPTER 2: YOU HAVE A SACRED BODY

OPENING TO GOD [5 MINUTES]
Begin with five minutes of silence followed by a prayer inviting God
to be with you and to guide your group conversations.

SOUL TRAINING [15-20 MINUTES]
If your group is larger than seven people, divide into small groups of
three or four before sharing answers to the following questions.

1. What version of moving did you try?

2. Did you find yourself more appreciative of your body? More
   aware of your body? More aware of the One who designed
   your body?

3. Did you notice your body movement producing hope in you?

4. Did you feel God's pleasure in your movement?

ENGAGING THE CHAPTER [25-45 MINUTES]
[*Note:* Be sure to think through which questions you especially want
to discuss.]

1. How did you feel as you read about how the author's pastor, Jeff,
   performs the sacrament of chrismation (anointing and blessing
   hands, feet, lips, etc.)?

2. How does your culture reflect the distortion that bodies are commodities? How does your own thinking reflect the distortion that
   bodies are commodities?

3. The author says that "our body needs our soul in order to live and
   move—to *animate* it. And our soul needs our body in order to reveal itself, to be made known, and to act." Can you describe your
   experience of daily life in this intertwinement?

4. Why does it matter whether you form your view of human beings
   on Adam or on Christ?

5. The section "Five Signs That Our Bodies Are Sacred" names the five parts of the Christian story (creation, incarnation, church, Eucharist, and glorification) that affirm the importance of the body. Which of those five give you the most encouragement about your body and appreciation of your body?

6. What is the significance to you that Christ ascended in bodily form?

ENGAGING SCRIPTURE [10-15 MINUTES]

Have a volunteer read the following Scripture aloud: Romans 6:13-14; Romans 7:17, 20-25; Romans 12:1; and 1 Corinthians 15:53-54.

1. How did Paul describe the conflict within us? Would it make sense to train the body for this conflict? Why or why not?

2. How does God rescue us from this conflict?

GO IN PEACE [5 MINUTES]

Spend a few minutes in silence imagining God's creation of you, sometimes called your conception. Imagine the creation of your body as God's purposeful design. Imagine the connection of your body to all other parts of your soul (mind, will, emotions, etc.) in your creation.

May you go in peace, grateful that your body is exactly the one that God purposed and created to be the good and beautiful you.

NEXT WEEK

In chapter three the theme is that you are wanted by God. The soul-training exercise will be *lectio divina* on Psalm 139 and Ephesians 2:10, which highlight God's desire for you.

CHAPTER 3: YOU ARE DESIRED

OPENING TO GOD [5 MINUTES]
Begin with five minutes of silence followed by an invitational prayer for God to be with you and to guide your group conversations.

SOUL TRAINING [15-20 MINUTES]
If your group is larger than seven people, divide into small groups of three or four. Here are some questions to help you share about your experiences with *lectio divina*.

1. What words or phrases stood out to you from the readings? How did that connect with your life?

2. Would anyone like to share what they wrote in their journal?

3. How did it affect you to take time to rest in God's interaction with you in this passage in the fourth step?

ENGAGING THE CHAPTER [25-45 MINUTES]
[*Note:* Be sure to think through which questions you especially want to discuss.]

You are not an accident, because your conception was an intentional, planned creation by God, no matter what was going on with your parents. God designed you in just the way he wanted you to be, and then he looked at you and said, "You are very good." God continues to look at you and say, "You are very good." He is so happy with his creation of you!

1. Have you ever felt like you were an "accident"? Where are you in your journey of receiving the reality of being wanted and designed by the Creator of the universe?

2. Adrian van Kaam uses the analogy of a seed to express how you are designed by God. The seed is your form, planned and created by the "Divine Forming Mystery." What does that name for God (Divine Forming Mystery) that Van Kaam uses say about you? How do you think and feel about being designed?

3. How is Christ's incarnation the source of our validation?

4. Did Dawn's illumination about the blade of grass speak to you in any way?

5. Poetry is meant to be read aloud. Ask someone to read the following poem, quoted in the chapter, while others just soak in the images painted with words. Then read it a second time, just listening to the words and not looking at them on the page.

Whisper to me again
How you formed me in my mother's womb,
Fashioned me over generations,
Over eons of unfolding of the earth
Until it could bear life
On its flaky crust, the dust
From which you formed our earthly frame
Endowing each of us with a name
Known to you alone.
Remind me how I dwelt in you,
My source and origin,
A call from eternity,
An archetype of life to be
Unique and irreplaceably
Your own.
(Adrian van Kaam)

ENGAGING SCRIPTURE [10-15 MINUTES]

Have a volunteer read the following Scriptures aloud, and then use the questions below as a discussion guide: Isaiah 43:6-7; Isaiah 49:16; and Revelation 2:17.

1. What does God inscribing you on the palm of his hands mean?

2. If you had to make a wild guess, what do you think is written on your white stone?

GO IN PEACE [5 MINUTES]

You are invited to pray (if you dare) what Macrina Weiderkehr prayed so eloquently:

> O God, help me to believe the truth about myself, no matter how beautiful.

May you go in peace, knowing that a good and beautiful God made you good and beautiful as well.

NEXT WEEK

In chapter four the theme is that you are loved by God. The soul-training exercise will be breath prayers, which are short, meditative, repetitive prayers in which we affirm a truth about the love of God.

CHAPTER 4: YOU ARE LOVED

OPENING TO GOD [5 MINUTES]

Begin with five minutes of silence followed by an invitational prayer for God to be with you and to guide your group conversations.

SOUL TRAINING [15-20 MINUTES]

If your group is larger than seven people, divide into small groups of three or four before sharing about your experiences with breath prayer.

1. What did you learn about God or yourself in this practice?

2. What affirmations did you use in your breath prayer practice? Which did you find the most encouraging to you?

ENGAGING THE CHAPTER [25-45 MINUTES]

[*Note:* Be sure to think through which questions you especially want to discuss.]

1. What did you learn from the author's story about how his dad responded to his amazing basketball score of fifty-one points? What chords did it strike with you in your own story? In what

ways has the relationship between you and God been shaped by your parents or other caregivers?

2. What are other common sources (besides parents) that teach us, often without words, that love is conditional? Would you like to share from the influences on your own journey?

3. Ask someone to read the poem aloud by Teresa of Ávila on page 73. What speaks to you in her words?

4. What do you think about the Peter van Breeman quote that says that God cannot divide his love as we do, because "God is perfectly one, the perfect unity. We *have* love, but God *is* love. His love is not an activity, it is his whole self"? What is the significance of Breeman's thoughts?

5. Is it hard for you to, as William Blake said, "bear the beams of love"? How does Jesus help us with our capacity?

6. How important is it in your other love relationships to receive affirmation? Does the following make sense to you—God not only initiates love toward you in the beginning, but God is the continual initiator of affirmations of his love for you?

7. How did Michael the counselor help the author look at his dad's comments about his feet in a different way? Is there a story in your own life that might be retold?

ENGAGING SCRIPTURE [10-15 MINUTES]
Have a volunteer read the following Scripture aloud: 2 Corinthians 3:18 and 2 Corinthians 4:6.

1. How did Paul describe transformation in the first verse?

2. If looking in the mirror at the glory of the Lord means gazing upon the face of Christ, what does this mean for you in your sanctification process? How does this connect to love?

GO IN PEACE [5 MINUTES]

You are invited to gaze at the face of Christ for a few minutes of silence.

May you go in peace, knowing that you are not your own source, but God in Christ loves you with a love that is beyond width, beyond depth, beyond length, and beyond breadth, surpassing even knowledge, that you might be filled to overflowing with the love of Christ.

NEXT WEEK

In chapter five the theme is that you are made for God. The soul-training exercise of worship will let your soul experience the connection to God for which it longs.

CHAPTER 5: YOU ARE MADE FOR GOD

OPENING TO GOD [5 MINUTES]

Begin with five minutes of silence followed by a prayer inviting God to be with you and to guide your group conversations.

SOUL TRAINING [15-20 MINUTES]

If your group is larger than seven people, divide into small groups of three or four.

1. Share about any personal worship experiences. What did you do? How were you ravished or transported into God's holy presence?

2. Were you able to prepare your heart, mind, and soul for corporate worship, as the author suggested? If so, how did that affect your experience of worship?

ENGAGING THE CHAPTER [25-45 MINUTES]

[*Note:* Be sure to think through which questions you especially want to discuss.]

1. You are invited to describe any memorable human encounters you have had with the transcendent God through the "aesthetic

perception, that glimpse of radiance, mystery, and meaning we see in a work of art or in the natural world," as Balthasar portrayed and the author described when he listened to Pachelbel's Canon.

2. What have you sought to satisfy your longing for God with in the past? Did something other than God satisfy that deep longing for the transcendent? What graces did you experience to move you more toward God?

3. The author states several times that our longings for things like money, power, sex, and approval are longings for the transcendent, but ultimately do not satisfy because they are not truly transcendent. Have you felt this longing, or experienced this dissatisfaction? If so, explain.

4. What role have summit experiences played in your connection with the transcendent dimension?

5. How do you connect with the transcendent dimension in the web of everydayness?

ENGAGING SCRIPTURE [10-15 MINUTES]
Have a volunteer read Romans 8:15-16 and John 4:24 aloud.

1. How would you describe the experience of the Holy Spirit connecting with your spirit in your own life?

2. What is worship?

GO IN PEACE [5 MINUTES]
You are invited to spend a few moments in silence, as a child of God simply letting your spirit connect to the Holy Spirit.

May you go in peace, and may you dwell in the house of the Lord all the days of your life, beholding the beauty of the Lord and meditating in his temple (Psalm 27:4 NASB).

NEXT WEEK

In chapter six the theme is that we are forgiven, *once for all*, and that we do not have to live a frantic life of confession to make sure we are forgiven for each jot and tittle of our sins. The soul-training exercise of laying your burden down will train you to walk in newness of life.

CHAPTER 6: YOU ARE FORGIVEN

OPENING TO GOD [5 MINUTES]
Begin with five minutes of silence followed by an invitational prayer for God to be with you and to guide your group conversations.

SOUL TRAINING [15-20 MINUTES]
If your group is larger than seven people, divide into small groups of three or four before sharing your answers to the following questions.

1. How did it feel to carry the weight of your sins around?

2. How did it feel to lay your burdens down?

3. How was it to walk with Jesus without your sins in the way?

ENGAGING THE CHAPTER [25-45 MINUTES]
[*Note:* Be sure to think through which questions you especially want to discuss.]

1. Do you live with unmanageable sin debt? Are you burdened by continual confession to keep your accounts clear with God? Does this keep you from living in the reality of the resurrection?

2. On page 106 the author says he had to pull his car over when he heard this on the radio: "Until you rest in the finality of the cross, you will never experience the reality of the resurrection." What does that mean? Do we too often think of the cross as the final thing rather than the beginning of victorious life in Christ? How so?

3. Have you ever entered into an intense battle to keep the law comprehensively? How did that go? What was the problem you ran up against?

4. How is our sin problem dealt a final blow? After contrasting the sacrificial system with the cross, we read on page 112 that "Jesus didn't cover up sin; . . . he took away sin." Is there still a need to confess our sins to be forgiven? Why or why not?

5. On page 114 we read that "confession is of great value." What is the value of confession if not for forgiveness? Please explain.

6. If it is true that we have forgiveness of sin once for all, doesn't that give us license to sin?

ENGAGING SCRIPTURE [10-15 MINUTES]

Have a volunteer read the following Scriptures aloud.

> Since the law has only a shadow of the good things to come and not the true form of these realities, it can never, by the same sacrifices that are continually offered year after year, make perfect those who approach. (Hebrews 10:1)

> For it was fitting for us to have such a high priest, holy, innocent, undefiled, separated from sinners, and exalted above the heavens; who has no daily need, like those high priests, to offer up sacrifices, first for His own sins and then for the *sins* of the people, because He did this **once for all** *time* when He offered up Himself. (Hebrews 7:26-27 NASB, emphasis added)

Now please read in unison the following paraphrases of these Scriptures while giving thanks in your heart:

> *The law can never make me perfect by continually offered sacrifices. But Christ took care of my sins **once for all time** by offering himself.*

Have another volunteer read Jeremiah 31:33 aloud, and then answer the questions below.

1. What does it mean for God's law to be written on your heart? Does that change your desires toward sin?

2. What is the relational outcome of that law within you?

GO IN PEACE [5 MINUTES]

Reflect silently for a few minutes on the look of God upon Jesus on the cross. Imagine the look of God's love toward the sacrifice of his Son being so great that it eclipsed the sins that Christ was dying for, and thus erased them forever.

May you go in peace, knowing that you have a clean erasure of all your sins, even the ones you never confess.

NEXT WEEK

In chapter seven the theme is that you have been made alive in Christ. The soul-training exercise will help you enter the kingdom as a little child, full of life, joy, and curiosity. Please note that this exercise may take several hours, or even a whole day if you choose.

CHAPTER 7: YOU HAVE BEEN MADE ALIVE

OPENING TO GOD [5 MINUTES]

Begin with five minutes of silence followed by a prayer inviting God to be with you and to guide your group conversations.

SOUL TRAINING [15-20 MINUTES]

If your group is larger than seven people, divide into small groups of three or four.

You are invited to share how the exercise of being childlike went for you.

1. Did you have resistance to this exercise? How were you able to overcome that resistance?

2. The author says that "your embodied soul was not made for sin, but for happiness and fun and excitement." Did this exercise put

you in a place of experiencing happiness, fun, or excitement? Would you like to share specifics?

3. Did your soul seem a little lighter or freer after your experiences of childlike responses or curiosity? Please elaborate.

ENGAGING THE CHAPTER [25-45 MINUTES]
[*Note:* Be sure to think through which questions you especially want to discuss.]

1. After Stan finally realized that he was a butterfly, he said "Now the gospel makes sense. It is not about what we do for God. It is what God has done for us" (p. 123). What about you? Are you, even some of the time, living as though it's all about what you do for God? If so, what is that like for you? Or are you living in the gospel that it's all about what God has done for you? If so, what's that like for you?

2. The author says on page 124 that a gospel that focuses only on escaping death "is not *wrong,* it is just *incomplete.*" Think back to your conversion story or maybe the first time you were presented with the gospel. Was it an incomplete gospel? What was missing? How did that affect your journey?

3. How does the resurrection apply to your everyday life?

4. What's your response to this statement on page 129: "You and I come premade to be conformed to the image of Christ"? What effect does it have on your day-to-day journey that you are already "shaped" for becoming like Jesus?

5. What is the image of God in you? How would you support that from Scripture? How do you become conformed to that image?

6. What are two aspects of the easy yoke? Have you experienced either of them? You are invited to share your experience with either.

ENGAGING SCRIPTURE [10-15 MINUTES]

Have a volunteer read Ephesians 2:4-6 and 2 Corinthians 5:17 aloud. Then use the questions below to discuss these passages.

1. According to these Scriptures, why is it unnecessary to walk around as a "forgiven dead person"?

2. What seems to bring about Christ living in you according to these Scriptures?

3. What might life be like if you lived in the reality of Christ in you and you in Christ?

GO IN PEACE [5 MINUTES]

You are invited to live the resurrection life because "the Spirit of him who raised Jesus from the dead is living in you" (Romans 8:11 NIV).

May you go in peace, knowing that the reality of resurrection life is given to you freely as a gift.

NEXT WEEK

The theme of chapter eight is that you are made holy because Christ dwells and delights in you. The soul-training exercise of "saying yes to God always" will flow out of the reality of the resurrected life of Christ living in you.

CHAPTER 8: YOU HAVE BEEN MADE HOLY

OPENING TO GOD [5 MINUTES]

Begin with five minutes of silence followed by a prayer inviting God to be with you and to guide your group conversations.

SOUL TRAINING [15-20 MINUTES]

If your group is larger than seven people, divide into small groups of three or four before sharing about the following questions.

1. Did you sense an area where God is calling you to say yes to him?

2. How was it to just connect to God as tree roots draw nourishment from the earth and river?

3. What specific graces did you receive from connecting to God?

ENGAGING THE CHAPTER [25-45 MINUTES]

[*Note:* Be sure to think through which questions you especially want to discuss.]

1. Why do you think the "I'm just a sinner, saved by grace" narrative is such a prevalent one? Has it had much power in your own life? What kind of fruit does it seem to produce?

2. Is the narrative "By the grace of God, I have been made holy" new for you? Does it seem more in sync with your soul's longing for purity? How would you explain this narrative?

3. The author states that "this sanctification, this holiness we receive by grace, is not merely positional but is 'accomplished'" (p. 146). What difference do you see in these two ideas, and why does it matter?

4. The author states that "what Christ has done compels us to what we can and now must do" (p. 148). What has Christ done? How is that compelling?

5. Since your identity in Christ is "a saint made holy by Jesus," what brings consonance with that identity? What brings dissonance? Does your own experience validate this dynamic?

6. The pride-form, the desire to be God (original sin), resists grace and puts our soul in a state of dissonance and war within. How can our pride give way to holiness?

ENGAGING SCRIPTURE [10-15 MINUTES]

Have a volunteer read the following Scriptures aloud: 1 Corinthians 15:22; Ephesians 5:8; 1 John 1:7; Colossians 3:4; and Galatians 2:19-20.

1. What do these verses on light and life have to do with relational holiness?

2. What kind of hope do these verses give us for being conformed to the holy character of Jesus?

GO IN PEACE [5 MINUTES]

For a few minutes of silence, you are invited to rest in Christ whose Spirit dwells in you, making you holy.

May you go in peace, empowered to be holy as he is holy, because he lives in you.

NEXT WEEK

In chapter nine the focus is on your sacred story. The soul-training exercise of letting God retell a part of your story will help you see yourself from God's perspective.

CHAPTER 9: YOU HAVE A SACRED STORY

OPENING TO GOD [5 MINUTES]

Begin with five minutes of silence followed by a prayer inviting God to be with you and to guide your group conversations.

SOUL TRAINING [15-20 MINUTES]

If your group is larger than seven people, divide into small groups of three or four before sharing answers to the following questions.

1. What did you learn about yourself as you looked more closely at your story?

2. What did you learn about God as you looked more closely at your story?

ENGAGING THE CHAPTER [25-45 MINUTES]

[*Note:* Be sure to think through which questions you especially want to discuss.]

1. What is meant by the term "circle of origin"? What is your circle of origin?

2. The author says on page 163 that "Mom and Dad not only give us their DNA, they also give us our sense of worth." In what ways did you get both DNA and a sense of worth from your parents or other primary caregiver?

3. Is anyone's circle of origin also a circle of sufficiency? Why or why not? What is the only circle of sufficiency? Can you share your personal experience with the only sufficient circle?

4. What are the two ways others harm us? Did you experience either of those in a way that shaped your soul? Please share as much as you are comfortable.

5. What does it mean to *ultimize* parts of your story? What does it mean to minimize your story? Do you see any examples in your own life? If you feel comfortable, you are invited to share your example.

6. What does it mean to experience healing of your story? Why do we sometimes resist that? How did God begin the healing of Hope's story? Have you received some healing of your story? What has that looked like?

ENGAGING SCRIPTURE [10-15 MINUTES]

Have a volunteer read the following Scriptures aloud. Then discuss the question(s) that follow each selection.

Reader, please include this brief introduction in your reading aloud:

This first verse is probably one of the most frequently quoted Scriptures, especially in times of tragedy, and perhaps our over-familiarity with it makes it hard for us to hear the living and active truth of this amazing promise. But open your heart to hearing it afresh.

1. "And we know that God causes all things to work together for good to those who love God, to those who are called according to *His* purpose" (Romans 8:28 NASB).

   How might this truth apply to your sacred story?

2. "For I am convinced that neither death, nor life, nor angels, nor principalities, nor things present, nor things to come, nor powers, nor height, nor depth, nor any other created thing will be able to separate us from the love of God that is in Christ Jesus our Lord" (Romans 8:38-39 NASB).

   How might this verse encourage you regarding the difficult elements of your story?

GO IN PEACE [5 MINUTES]

The Trinity encircles you with all that you need, even if you didn't get it from your family. The Trinity heals your soul of any inflicted harm. You are invited to spend a few minutes silently resting in the sufficiency of the circle of the Trinity.

May you go in peace, knowing that God looks upon you with eyes brighter than the sun, and that he has written your unique name on a white stone, a name that is not erased by your story, but showcased by your story—for God is the shepherd and guardian of your soul, preserving your identity as you live out your sacred story.

NEXT WEEK

In chapter ten the theme is that you are called. The soul-training exercise of listening to the verbs of your true self will give you insight into the nature of your calling.

CHAPTER 10: YOU ARE CALLED

OPENING TO GOD [5 MINUTES]

Begin with five minutes of silence followed by a prayer inviting God to be with you and to guide your group conversations.

SOUL TRAINING [15-20 MINUTES]
If your group is larger than seven people, divide into small groups of three or four before sharing answers to the following questions.

1. How was it to listen to the verbs of your life?
2. Would you like to share your list of fifteen verbs, seven verbs, or your final four verbs?
3. What were the sentences or phrases you crafted?

ENGAGING THE CHAPTER [25-45 MINUTES]
[*Note*: Be sure to think through which questions you especially want to discuss.]

1. The author states that there are two callings, your "capital *C* calling" and your "small *c* callings." What are your thoughts about these two callings and about how they are related?
2. What are the two parts of Buechner's famous formula for discerning your calling? Do they shed any light on your vocational calling? Have you found any other helpful principles or tools in your own discernment process that you'd like to share?
3. The story of Ray Anderson concludes with the idea that our destiny can be found in discovering the thing we would like to do until our final day on earth. Have you been able to discover your own destiny?
4. How has your story shaped your calling?
5. What is the seasonal dimension to one's calling? Please share if you have experienced seasonal shifts in your calling.

ENGAGING SCRIPTURE [10-15 MINUTES]
Have a volunteer read Exodus 31:1-11 aloud.

1. What do you notice about vocational calling in this passage?
2. How is Bezalel's "filling" described? Is there any comfort or encouragement to you in this aspect of Bezalel's calling? Please explain.

GO IN PEACE [5 MINUTES]

You are invited to take a few minutes of silence to notice how God has filled you and equipped you for your vocational calling.

May you go in peace, knowing that the Divine Forming Mystery has designed you uniquely and perfectly to flourish in whatever he calls you unto.

NEXT WEEK

In chapter eleven the theme is that you will be glorified. The soul-training exercise of celebration will sanctify some time and space and matter to help you rejoice with gladness over God and his goodness.

CHAPTER 11: YOU WILL BE GLORIFIED

OPENING TO GOD [5 MINUTES]

Begin with five minutes of silence followed by a prayer inviting God to be with you and to guide your group conversations.

SOUL TRAINING [15-20 MINUTES]

If your group is larger than seven people, divide into small groups of three or four before sharing about the following questions.

1. How did you celebrate? What were the highlights?

2. Did the future enter into your present through your celebration?

ENGAGING THE CHAPTER [25-45 MINUTES]

[*Note:* Be sure to think through which questions you especially want to discuss.]

1. What does the author mean when he says, "Nonexistence is unconscionable"?

2. How do miracles foreshadow the general resurrection?

3. O'Donohue says that there must be "joy in bringing the bright essence of a life's harvest into eternity." Revelation 21:24 says that "the kings

of the earth will bring their glory," or splendor, into the new Jerusalem (heaven come down to earth). What harvest from your life, what splendor, can you imagine that you would bring into eternity?

4. How does your heart connect with the inconsolable secret?

5. The author states that, wonderfully, "glorification frees us from the *presence* of sin." And also that "God designed you and me with incredible capacities to dream, imagine, and create." If you add together your God-created, incredible capacities and freedom from the presence of sin, what do you get? Please share some possibilities. What do you hope God assigns you to do?

ENGAGING SCRIPTURE [10-15 MINUTES]

Have a volunteer read the following Scriptures aloud: 1 Thessalonians 4:13-14; 2 Corinthians 4:16-18; and Colossians 3:3-4.

1. Paul informs us that we grieve with hope. Bonhoeffer said that God leaves the emptiness (grief) "precisely unfilled and thus helps us preserve—even in pain—the authentic relationship," but our lovely memories are "but a hidden treasure of which one can always be certain" (hope). How is it that we experience both grief and hope at the same time?

2. What is the *basis* for our hope amid our grief, even as we face our own death?

3. What image comes to mind when you think of being revealed in glory with Christ? Can you describe what you see?

GO IN PEACE [5 MINUTES]

You are invited to think of a specific person (a friend or family member) and imagine for a few moments of silence what their future glorification could be like. Let your heart swell with joy on their behalf.

May you go in peace, comforted and strengthened by the certainty of a good future. As you are in this history, you will also be in the new heavens and the new earth: the good and beautiful you!

Notes

Introduction

p. 2   *To remind myself*: David Brooks, *The Second Mountain* (New York: Random House, 2019), xx.

p. 4   *I must become the unique person*: Adrian van Kaam, *On Being Yourself* (Denville, NJ: Dimension Books, 1972), 8.

Chapter 1: You Have a Soul

p. 12   *There was this primitive core*: Parker Palmer, "The Soul in Depression," February 4, 2021, in *On Being*, produced by Krista Tippett, podcast, https://onbeing.org/programs/the-soul-in-depression/.

p. 13   *The twentieth century has been called*: Adam Curtis, dir., *The Century of the Self* (London: BBC and RDF Media, 2002).

p. 13   *A few years ago*: John Ortberg, *Soul Keeping: Caring for the Most Important Part of You* (Grand Rapids, MI: Zondervan, 2014), chap. 2, Kindle loc. 207.

p. 13   *James Hillman, renowned psychologist*: James Hillman and Michael Ventura, *We've Had a Hundred Years of Psychotherapy—And the World's Getting Worse* (San Francisco: HarperOne, 1993).

p. 15   *Your soul weighs nothing*: John Ortberg, *You Have a Soul* (Grand Rapids, MI: Zondervan, 2014), front cover.

p. 15   *I had given up on life*: Taylor Momsen, "Taylor Momsen on Music, Mental Health and Child Stardom," *People Magazine*, March 1, 2021, www.scribd.com/article/495218010/Taylor-Momsen-On-Music-Mental-Health-Child-Stardom.

p. 16   *Your embodied soul "is the 'you'"*: Ruth Haley Barton, *Strengthening the Soul of Your Leadership: Seeking God in the Crucible of Ministry* (Downers Grove, IL: InterVarsity Press, 2008), 13.

p. 17   *We shall search the Old and New*: Karl Barth, Thomas F. Torrance, and Geoffrey William Bromiley, *Church Dogmatics* (Edinburgh: T&T Clark, 1956), III/2, 433.

p. 17   *The soul is the "whole person"*: Ray Anderson, *On Being Human* (Grand Rapids, MI: Eerdmans, 1982), 210.

p. 22   *The soul's infinite capacity to desire*: Ortberg, *You Have a Soul*, 9.

p. 24   *All that I needed*: Thomas O. Chisholm, "Great Is Thy Faithfulness," *The United Methodist Hymnal* (Nashville, TN: United Methodist Publishing House, 1989), hymn no. 140.

p. 24   *My sin—oh, the bliss:* Horatio Spafford, "It Is Well with My Soul," verse 3, 1873, www.spaffordhymn.com.

p. 26   *The church Fathers often spoke:* Richard J. Foster, *Celebration of Discipline* (San Francisco: HarperCollins, 1978), 27.

Chapter 2: You Have a Sacred Body

p. 33   *Prison for the soul:* D. N. Sedley, *Plato's Cratylus* (Cambridge, NY: Cambridge University Press, 2003), 400c.

p. 35   *The body is the instrument:* Saint John Chrysostom, *Homilies on Genesis,* trans. Robert C. Hill, The Fathers of the Church 74 (Washington, DC: Catholic University of America Press, 1986), 14.5.

p. 35   *The body is not an accidental feature:* Jennifer M. Rosner, "Dishonorable Discharge: Our Soul and the World of Ritual Impurity," *Christianity Today,* May/June 2021.

p. 35   *Your mind can do more:* Annie Grace, *This Naked Mind* (New York: Random House, 2018), 43.

p. 39   *The Hebrew word* tov: Scot McKnight and Laura Barringer, *A Church Called Tov* (Carol Stream, IL: Tyndale House Publishers, 2020).

p. 40   *God took on a body:* Jean-Claude Larchet, *Theology of the Body* (Yonkers, NY: St. Vladimir's Seminary Press, 2016), 43.

p. 42   *While natural food is changed:* Saint Nicholas Cabasilas, *The Life in Christ* (Crestwood, NY: St. Vladimir's Seminary Press, 1974), 4.8.

p. 42   *John Calvin famously noted:* John Calvin, *Institutes of the Christian Religion* (Philadelphia: The Westminster Press, 1960), 4.17.32.

p. 43   *The body along with the soul:* Larchet, *Theology of the Body,* 94.

p. 43   *Glorification:* Larchet, *Theology of the Body,* 95.

p. 44   *For as God created the sky:* Pseudo-Macarius, Macarius, and Arthur J. Mason, *Fifty Spiritual Homilies of St. Macarius the Egyptian* (London: Society for Promoting Christian Knowledge, 1921).

p. 45   *Joel Clarkson:* Charlie Peacock, "Ordinary Life Is Crammed with Heaven," *Christianity Today,* February 16, 2021, www.christianitytoday.com/ct/2021 /march/sensing-god-joel-clarkson-ordinary-life-crammed-heaven.html.

p. 46   *God is loving you in these moments:* James Bryan Smith, *The Magnificent Story: Uncovering a Gospel of Beauty, Goodness, and Truth* (Downers Grove, IL: InterVarsity Press, 2017), 14.

p. 47   *God made me fast:* Hugh Hudson, dir., *Chariots of Fire* (London: Enigma Productions, 1981).

p. 47   *Physical activity influences:* Kelly McGonigal, *The Joy of Movement* (New York: Random House, 2019), 4-5.

p. 48   *Hope molecules:* McGonigal, *Joy of Movement,* 5.

p. 48   *Green exercise:* McGonigal, *Joy of Movement,* 255.

p. 48   *Prayer walking:* Adele Calhoun, *Spiritual Disciplines Handbook* (Downers Grove, IL: InterVarsity Press, 2005), 254.

Chapter 3: You Are Desired

p. 52   *Dawn's story*: Betsy McPeak, personal correspondence with author.

p. 52   *You are an accidentally united little lump*: Leo Tolstoy, *A Confession: The Gospel in Brief, and What I Believe*, trans. Aylmer Maude (London: Oxford University Press, 1958), 31.

p. 52   *The universe*: Richard Dawkins, *River Out of Eden* (New York: Basic Books, 1996), 133.

p. 52   *Your "soul" is make-believe*: Marshall Brain, *Marshall Brain's How Stuff Works* (Wiley Publishers, 2001).

p. 53   *There has been no advance*: Dallas Willard, *The Divine Conspiracy* (New York: HarperCollins, 1997), 8.

p. 53   *Thou madest man*: Alfred Lord Tennyson, "Prologue," *In Memoriam*, stanza 2. This poem is in the public domain.

p. 54   *A collection of atoms*: Andrew Crumey, "All and Nothing," *The Wall Street Journal*, March 13, 2021.

p. 55   *Divine Forming Mystery*: Adrian van Kaam, quoted in James C. Wilhoit, "Only God's Love Counts: Van Kaam's Formation Theology," *Journal of Spiritual Formation and Soul Care* 1, no. 2 (2008).

p. 57   *A good poem*: Marilyn Singer, "What Makes a Good Poem," Marilyn Singer official website, 2002, https://marilynsinger.net/what-makes-a-good-poem.

p. 57   *You are a divinely designed*: Dallas Willard, "Your Place in This World," Free Republic, May 10, 2005, https://freerepublic.com/focus/f-religion/1400713 /posts.

p. 58   *The Christmas hymn "O Holy Night"*: Adolphe Adam and Placide Cappeau, "O Holy Night," 1847.

p. 59   *Van Gogh's painting*: Kirstin Fawcett, "6 Valuable Works of Art Discovered in People's Attics and Garages," Mental Floss, September 8, 2017, www .mentalfloss.com/article/504146/6-valuable-works-art-discovered -peoples-attics-and-garages.

p. 60   *To be hidden in Christ*: Adrian van Kaam, *On Being Yourself* (Denville, NJ: Dimension Books, 1972), 176-77.

p. 60   *Rejecting our unique selves*: Adrian van Kaam, *In Search of Spiritual Identity* (Denville, NJ: Dimension Books, 1975), 140.

p. 61   *An invaluable, irreplaceable seed*: Mark Nepo, *The Endless Practice: Becoming Who You Were Born to Be* (New York: Atria Paperback, 2015), xviii.

p. 62   *O God, help me to believe*: Macrina Weiderkehr, *A Tree Full of Angels* (New York: HarperCollins, 1988).

p. 63   *Whisper to me again*: Adrian van Kaam, *Becoming Spiritually Mature* (Pittsburgh: Epiphany Association, 2007), 52.

Chapter 4: You Are Loved

p. 67   *Two questions haunt every human life*: Andy Crouch, *Strong and Weak: Embracing a Life of Love, Risk, and True Flourishing* (Downers Grove, IL: InterVarsity Press, 2016), 9.

p. 69   *sinners in the hands of an angry God*: The phrase "sinners in the hands of an angry God" is a reference to the title of the famous sermon by Jonathan Edwards.

p. 71   *Why do Christians hate*: Philip Yancey, *What's So Amazing About Grace?* (Grand Rapids, MI: Zondervan, 2002).

p. 72   *Jesus didn't die*: Brian Zahnd, *Sinners in the Hands of a Loving God* (Colorado Springs: WaterBrook, 2017), 85.

p. 72   *Under the tyranny*: Susan Annette Muto and Adrian van Kaam, *Tell Me Who I Am* (Denville, NJ: Dimension Books, 1977), 39.

p. 73   *When I first heard*: This poem by Teresa of Ávila, "He Desired Me So I Came Close," is a "rendering" by Daniel Ladinsky, from his book *Love Poems from God* (New York: Penguin Compass, 2002), 274, used by permission. Ladinsky has taken some liberties in his translations of Teresa's poem. Many of her poems were written (originally in Spanish) in her times of prayer, as dialogues between her and God. This version of the poem is not a word-for-word translation of one of Teresa's actual poems, but I found his version to speak directly to my soul with a powerful word about God's unquenchable love for us.

p. 74   *If we think of God*: Peter van Breeman, *As Bread That Is Broken* (Denville, NJ: Dimension Books, 1974), 14.

p. 75   *We love because*: Henri J. M. Nouwen, "Who Are We?" Audible lecture, Now You Know Media, Inc., 2017, www.audible.com/pd/Who-Are-We -Henri-Nouwen-on-Our-Christian-Identity-Audiobook/B074VGVX3S.

p. 76   *And we are put on earth*: William Blake, "The Little Black Boy."

p. 76   *Because of His measureless love*: Irenaeus, *Against Heresies*, 5.

p. 76   *Jesus needed*: Thomas Smail, *The Forgotten Father* (London: Hodder and Stoughton, 1980), 68.

p. 77   *In stark contrast to ourselves*: Trevor Hudson, *Discovering Our Spiritual Identity: Practices for God's Beloved* (Downers Grove, IL: InterVarsity Press, 2011), 26.

p. 77   *Turn stones into bread*: Henri J. M. Nouwen, *Here and Now* (New York: Crossroad, 2016), 99-100.

p. 78   *The beauty of the world*: Simone Weil, *Waiting for God* (New York: Routledge, 2010), 60.

p. 79   *When we wake up*: Søren Kierkegaard, quoted in James Bryan Smith and Richard J. Foster, *Devotional Classics* (San Francisco: HarperSanFrancisco, 1994), 107. Originally published in Søren Kierkegaard, *The Prayers of Kierkegaard,* ed. Perry LeFevre (Chicago: University of Chicago Press, 1956).

p. 79   *In this face*: Hans Urs von Balthasar, *Love Alone Is Credible* (San Francisco: Ignatius Press, 1963), 76.

Chapter 5: You Are Made for God

p. 87   *The essential starting point*: Quoted in Greg Wolfe, "Transfiguration," *Image* 27, 3-4.

p. 87   *Show and podcast called* Super Soul Sunday: Oprah Winfrey, *Super Soul Sunday*, www.oprah.com/app/super-soul-sunday.html.

p. 89   *Many people, lacking spirit*: Carl Jung, from his seminar on Nietzsche's *Zarathustra*, 1934–1939, https://drive.google.com/open?id=1L9mcYPdlAko1E afCOGUTbg-zW8ewXgVG.

p. 89   *Surfing for God*: Michael J. Cusick, *Surfing for God: Discovering the Divine Desire Beneath Sexual Struggle* (Nashville, TN: Thomas Nelson, 2012).

p. 91   *Love loves unto purity*: George MacDonald, "The Consuming Fire," sermon from *Unspoken Sermons*, First Series (Eureka, CA: Sunrise Books Publishers, 1988), 27.

p. 92   *Gifted disrupter*: Rebecca Letterman and Susan Muto, *Understanding Our Story* (Eugene, OR: Wipf & Stock, 2017), 209.

p. 93   *Thou hast made us for thyself*: Saint Augustine, *Confessions* (New York: Penguin Classics, 2008), 1, 1.5.

p. 93   *This craving*: Blaise Pascal, *Pensées* (New York: Penguin Books, 1966), 75.

p. 93   *"Spiritual" is not just something*: Dallas Willard, *The Divine Conspiracy* (San Francisco: HarperOne, 1997), 79.

p. 98   *Web of everydayness*: Adrian van Kaam, *Fundamental Formation* (New York: Crossroad, 1983), 153.

p. 98   *To see a world in a grain of sand*: William Blake, "Auguries of Innocence," lines 1-2.

p. 99   *Awe-filled attentive abiding*: Adrian van Kaam, *The Power of Appreciation* (Pittsburgh: Epiphany Association, 2004), 10.

p. 99   *living with "appreciative abandonment"*: Adrian van Kaam, *The Power of Appreciation* (Pittsburgh: Epiphany Association, 1993), 1.

p. 100   *Many people reach only incidentally*: Van Kaam, *Fundamental Formation*, 155-56.

p. 100   *May you come to accept*: John O'Donohue, "For Longing," in *To Bless the Space Between Us* (New York: Doubleday, 2008), 35-36.

p. 101   *The first fruit of love*: Thomas Watson, *All Things for Good* (1663; Carlisle, PA: The Banner of Truth Trust, 1986), 74.

p. 103   *An ordered way of acting*: Richard J. Foster, *Celebration of Discipline* (San Francisco: HarperCollins, 1978), 166.

p. 103   *Prepare for Sunday worship*: Foster, *Celebration*, 171.

Chapter 6: You Are Forgiven

p. 107   *Bob George radio ministry*: Bob George Ministries, https://bobgeorge.net/.

p. 115   *Wonderous exchange*: John Calvin, *Institutes of the Christian Religion* (Philadelphia: The Westminster Press, 1960), 4.17.2. This phrase, "wondrous exchange," is also in *The Epistle to Diognetus* 9, who was one of the Apostolic Fathers in the second century. So the term has a long history.

p. 115   *Endured it with joy*: Thomas F. Torrance, *Atonement: The Person and Work of Christ* (Downers Grove, IL: InterVarsity Press, 2009), 152, italics added.

p. 115   *While he [Luther] was describing the change*: John Wesley, *The Works of John Wesley*, vol. 18, *Journals and Diaries* (Nashville, TN: Abingdon Press, 1988) entry from May 24, 1738, italics added.

p. 117   *We can stop focusing on sin*: Bob George, *Classic Christianity* (Eugene, OR: Harvest House, 1989), 58.

p. 117   *My sin—oh, the bliss*: Horatio Spafford, "It Is Well with My Soul," verse 3, 1873, www.spaffordhymn.com.

p. 118   *Classic novel* Pilgrim's Progress: John Bunyan, *Pilgrim's Progress* (Oxford: Oxford University Press, 2003), sec. 3.

Chapter 7: You Have Been Made Alive

p. 124   *as Dallas Willard taught*: Dallas Willard, *The Divine Conspiracy* (New York: HarperCollins, 1998), 41.

p. 128   *Those who restore art*: Christopher Jobson, "The Meticulous 10-Month Restoration of a 355-Year-Old Painting at the Metropolitan Museum of Art," Colossal, June 30, 2015, www.thisiscolossal.com/2015/06/brun-painting-restoration-met/.

p. 131   *When we come to understand*: Leanne Payne, *Restoring the Christian Soul: Overcoming Barriers to Completion in Christ Through Healing Prayer* (Grand Rapids, MI: Baker Books, 2001), xiii.

p. 131   *The characteristic of the new birth*: Oswald Chambers, *My Utmost for His Highest* (Grand Rapids, MI: Discovery House, 2018), December 25 entry.

p. 131   *I would rather laugh*: Billy Joel, "Only the Good Die Young," *The Stranger* (Columbia Records, 1977), track 6.

p. 132   *The One who came*: Dallas Willard, *Spirit of the Disciplines* (San Francisco: Harper & Row, 1988), 79.

p. 132   *The greatest sin*: "New Bishop Willimon Displays Puckish Style: Hauerwas: 'It's a Sign We're Not Dead Yet,'" *Christian Century*, August 24, 2001, www.christiancentury.org/article/2004-08/new-bishop-willimon-displays-puckish-style.

p. 136   *Like the play of sunlight*: Mike Mason, *Champagne for the Soul: Rediscovering God's Gift of Joy* (Vancouver: Regent College Publishers, 2007), 69.

p. 137   *Just So Stories*: Rudyard Kipling, *Just So Stories for Little Children* (Leipzig: Tauchnitz, 1902).

p. 137   *The manna of joy*: Mason, *Champagne for the Soul*, 69.

Chapter 8: You Have Been Made Holy

p. 142   *When I was in seminary*: Søren Kierkegaard, *Purity of Heart Is to Will One Thing* (Merchant Books, 2013).

p. 144   *Paul's Corinthian correspondence*: Don J. Payne, *Already Sanctified* (Grand Rapids, MI: Baker Academic, 2020), 57.

p. 146   *Accomplished holiness*: Payne, *Already Sanctified*, 70.

p. 146   *The Christian is not just called*: Douglas J. Moo, *Epistle to the Romans* (Grand Rapids, MI: Eerdmans, 2015), 403. Also quoted in Payne, *Already Sanctified*, 130.

p. 150   *The imperative is not only*: Fleming Rutledge, *Crucifixion: Understanding the Death of Jesus Christ* (Grand Rapids, MI: Eerdmans, 2017), 558. Also quoted in Payne, *Already Sanctified*, 62.

p. 151   *To live in contradiction*: Payne, *Already Sanctified*, 129.

p. 152   *Original source of paranoid fears*: Adrian van Kaam, *Formative Spirituality*, vol. 6, *Transcendent Formation* (New York: Crossroad, 1995), 249.

p. 152   *The grace of God always kills*: Ray Sherman Anderson, *The Soul of Ministry: Forming Leaders for God's People* (Louisville, KY: Westminster John Knox Press, 1997), 47. Also Payne, *Already Sanctified*, 126.

p. 152   *The grace of rescue*: Rebecca Letterman and Susan Muto, *Understanding Our Story: The Life's Work and Legacy of Adrian van Kaam in the Field of Formative Spirituality* (Eugene, OR: Wipf and Stock, 2017), 47.

p. 152   *Attaining a sense of self-worth*: Susan Annette Muto and Adrian van Kaam, *Tell Me Who I Am* (Denville, NJ: Dimension Books, 1977), 35.

p. 153   *Grace is not opposed to effort*: Dallas Willard, *The Great Omission: Reclaiming Jesus's Essential Teachings on Discipleship* (New York: HarperOne, 2007), 61.

p. 153   *Love loves unto purity*: George MacDonald, "The Consuming Fire," sermon from *Unspoken Sermons*, First Series (Eureka, CA: Sunrise Books Publishers, 1988), 27.

p. 155   *Here and now is where we must listen*: Adrian van Kaam, "Say Yes Always," no. 4, *Becoming Spiritually Mature*, Epiphany Video Series (Pittsburgh: Epiphany Association, 2007).

Chapter 9: You Have a Sacred Story

p. 161   *Each of us is conceived*: Rebecca Letterman and Susan Muto, *Understanding Our Story: The Life's Work and Legacy of Adrian van Kaam in the Field of Formative Spirituality* (Eugene, OR: Wipf & Stock, 2017), 27.

p. 162   *Circle of origin*: Dallas Willard, *Renovation of the Heart* (Colorado Springs: NavPress, 2002), 180.

p. 162   *Sociohistorical dimension*: This is a term used by Fr. Adrian van Kaam. It is explained in the book and video series *Becoming Spiritually Mature* (Pittsburgh: Epiphany Association, 2007).

p. 162   *It plays a markedly formative role*: Letterman and Muto, *Understanding Our Story*, 26.

p. 162   *They who passed away long ago*: Rainer Maria Rilke, *Letters to a Young Poet* (New York: Vintage Books, 1984), 86.

p. 163   *Our circle of origin*: Willard, *Renovation of the Heart*, 36.

p. 163   *Someone is for us*: Willard, *Renovation of the Heart*, 179.

p. 163   *When you are dejected*: John of Kronstadt is credited with this quote, but the source is unknown.

p. 163   *We assault others*: Willard, *Renovation of the Heart*, 182.

p. 166   *A British documentary*: Michael Apted, dir., *56 Up* (London: ITV Studios, 2012).

p. 166   *We are the beneficiaries*: David Brooks, from a talk he gave at the Leadership Conference held by the Murdock Trust, Dec. 3, 2020.

p. 167   *It is a lifelong task*: Adrian van Kaam, *Fundamental Formation* (New York: Crossroad, 1983), 94-95.

p. 167   *In his book* A Grace Disguised: Gerald Sittser, *A Grace Disguised* (Nashville, TN: Zondervan, 2004), 45.

p. 169   *Form a massive matrix*: Letterman and Muto, *Understanding Our Story*, 27.

p. 169   *Love comes to us from God*: Willard, *Renovation of the Heart*, 183.

p. 171   *The reversal of traumas*: Adrian van Kaam, *Foundations of Christian Formation* (Pittsburgh: Epiphany Association, 2004), 42.

p. 172   *When we have the courage*: Brené Brown, *Dare to Lead* (New York: Random House, 2018), 240.

p. 173   *We believe something*: Willard, *Renovation of the Heart*.

p. 173   *You construct your understanding*: Curt Thompson, *Anatomy of the Soul* (Carol Stream, IL: Tyndale House, 2010), 77.

Chapter 10: You Are Called

p. 185   *Be who God meant you to be*: Saint Catherine of Siena, *Saint Catherine of Siena as Seen in Her Letters*, ed. Vida Dutton Scudder (London: J.M. Dent & Co., 1905), "Letter to Stefano Maconi" (1376).

p. 186   *The best advice I can give*: This quote from Frederick Buechner, as I wrote it in my notebook, was something he said often and wrote about. In fact, a later devotional that consists of his writings is titled *Listening to Your Life* (San Francisco: HarperSanFrancisco, 1992).

p. 187   *By and large a good rule*: Frederick Buechner, *Wishful Thinking* (New York: Harper & Row, 1973), 95.

p. 188   *My father had not attached*: Ray Anderson, *Unspoken Wisdom: Truths My Father Taught Me* (Eugene, OR: Wipf and Stock, 2013), 18.

p. 193   *Within you is a fathomless reservoir*: Dick Staub, *About You: Fully Human, Fully Alive* (San Francisco: Jossey-Bass, 2010), 184.

p. 193   *Fun exercise where we notice*: Jim Banks, *One Calling, One Ministry* (Campbellsville, KY: House of Healing Ministries, 2012), Kindle loc. 1099.

p. 193   *What we really want to do*: Julia Cameron, *The Artist's Way* (New York: TarcherPerigee, 1992), 108.

p. 195   *God's creative call is revealed*: Adrian van Kaam, *In Search of Spiritual Identity* (Denville, NJ: Dimension Books, 1975), 143.

Chapter 11: You Will Be Glorified

p. 199   *I don't believe in Heaven*: Scot McKnight, *The Heaven Promise* (Colorado Springs: WaterBrook, 2015), 144.

p. 200   *Jesus abolished death*: Dallas Willard, *The Divine Conspiracy* (San Francisco: HarperCollins, 1998), 84.

p. 201   *When You're old enough to speak*: Penny and Sparrow, "Smitten, Pt. 2,", Andy Baxter and Kyle Jahnke, *Wendigo*, I Love You, 2017.

p. 202   *Reliability of the promise of heaven*: McKnight, *Heaven Promise*, 24.

p. 203   *While the knowing of the mind*: John O'Donohue, *Beauty: The Invisible Embrace* (New York: Harper Perennial, 2005), 205-6.

p. 203   *For your soul*: O'Donohue, *Beauty*, 208.

p. 204   *Glory means good report with God*: C. S. Lewis, *The Weight of Glory* (New York: Simon & Schuster, 1996), 36.

p. 204   *It may be possible*: Lewis, *Weight of Glory*, 39.

p. 209   *There is nothing that can replace*: Dietrich Bonhoeffer, *Letters and Papers from Prison*, vol. 8, *Works* (Minneapolis: Fortress, 2009), letter no. 89.

p. 210   *Grief is a small penalty*: John Pavlovitz, "Grief Is the Tax on Loving People," John Pavlovitz blog, August 24, 2019, https://johnpavlovitz.com/2019/08/24/grief-is-the-tax-on-loving-people/.

p. 212   *Celebration is at the heart*: Richard J. Foster, *Celebration of Discipline* (San Francisco: HarperCollins, 1978), 190.

p. 212   *God is the most joyous*: Willard, *Divine Conspiracy*, 62.

p. 212   *Jubilee of the Spirit*: Foster, *Celebration*, 190.

p. 213   *A way of engaging*: Adele Calhoun, *Spiritual Disciplines Handbook* (Downers Grove, IL: InterVarsity Press, 2005), 2.

Also from James Bryan Smith

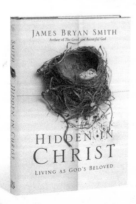

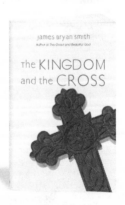